T0311770

Cambridge Elements ☰

Elements in Contentious Politics
edited by
David S. Meyer
University of California, Irvine
Suzanne Staggenborg
University of Pittsburgh

THE EVOLUTION OF AUTHORITARIANISM AND CONTENTIOUS ACTION IN RUSSIA

Bogdan Mamaev
Griffith University

CAMBRIDGE
UNIVERSITY PRESS

Shaftesbury Road, Cambridge CB2 8EA, United Kingdom

One Liberty Plaza, 20th Floor, New York, NY 10006, USA

477 Williamstown Road, Port Melbourne, VIC 3207, Australia

314–321, 3rd Floor, Plot 3, Splendor Forum, Jasola District Centre,
New Delhi – 110025, India

103 Penang Road, #05–06/07, Visioncrest Commercial, Singapore 238467

Cambridge University Press is part of Cambridge University Press & Assessment,
a department of the University of Cambridge.

We share the University's mission to contribute to society through the pursuit of
education, learning and research at the highest international levels of excellence.

www.cambridge.org
Information on this title: www.cambridge.org/9781009560689

DOI: 10.1017/9781009560672

© Bogdan Mamaev 2024

First published 2024

A catalogue record for this publication is available from the British Library.

ISBN 978-1-009-56068-9 Hardback
ISBN 978-1-009-56065-8 Paperback
ISSN 2633-3570 (online)
ISSN 2633-3562 (print)

The Evolution of Authoritarianism and Contentious Action in Russia

Elements in Contentious Politics

DOI: 10.1017/9781009560672
First published online: May 2024

Bogdan Mamaev
Griffith University

Author for correspondence: Bogdan Mamaev, b.mamaev@griffith.edu.au

Abstract: This Element examines the evolution of authoritarianism in Russia from 2011 to 2023, focusing on its impact on contentious action. It argues that the primary determinant of contention, at both federal and regional levels, is authoritarian innovation characterized by reactive and proactive repression. Drawing on Russian legislation, reports from human rights organizations, media coverage, and a novel dataset of contentious events created from user-generated reports on Twitter using computational techniques, the Element contributes to the understanding of contentious politics in authoritarian regimes, underscoring the role of authoritarianism and its innovative responses in shaping contentious action.

Keywords: authoritarianism, contentious politics, repression, protest, Russia

ISBNs: 9781009560689 (HB), 9781009560658 (PB), 9781009560672 (OC)
ISSNs: 2633-3570 (online), 2633-3562 (print)

Contents

1 Introduction

In 2011–2012, Russia witnessed massive rallies following the State Duma election, which many viewed as fraudulent (Bader et al., 2014; Enikolopov et al., 2012). Although electoral fraud was not a new phenomenon in Russian politics, the public's response to this particular instance was unprecedented in its scale, drawing a large number of participants and sparking protests across the country (Chaisty & Whitefield, 2013). Some observers celebrated this surge in participation as a step toward the emergence of a robust civil society in Russia, while others optimistically interpreted it as the dawn of a new era in Russian democracy, signaling a shift toward greater political rights and civil liberties (Cheskin & March, 2015; Robertson, 2013). Participants in these rallies articulated their demands, calling for fair elections, a free Russia, and the departure of Vladimir Putin.

While the 2011–2012 events sparked growing expectations for a democratic transformation in Russia, such change never materialized (Trenin et al., 2012; Wolchik, 2012). Following the 2012 presidential election, the regime responded with intensified repression and an array of new measures to contain public discontent. This period marked a significant infringement on civil liberties through its crackdown on opposition and the introduction of repressive legislation (Libman, 2017). Bolotnaya Square, which had emerged as a focal point for the 2011–2012 rallies, became a lasting symbol of political persecution, as many participants faced detention and criminal charges in the years that followed. The government enacted laws penalizing unauthorized mass gatherings, established website blocklists, and expanded the definitions of terms like state treason, espionage, and foreign agents. The situation was further exacerbated after the invasion of Ukraine, heralding a surge in propaganda, nationalist rhetoric, and redefinitions of what constituted criminal offenses.

Yet despite the regime's implementation of repressive measures, contentious events continued to play their role in Russia's political landscape. To ensure its dominance in contentious politics and respond to contentious claims, the regime continued to innovate its strategies. Major protests, including rallies against the annexation of Crimea in 2014, objections to the 2016 parliamentary election results, anticorruption demonstrations in 2017, and pension reform in 2018, coincided with extensive political changes in new regulations. Rosgvardia, an internal security army, became a direct instrument of presidential power, entrusted with the authority to suppress, detain, and prosecute (Galeotti, 2021). Presidential terms were extended, and opposition media slowly vanished as a result of the laws targeting undesired organizations and foreign agents. The mass rallies in Bolotnaya Square over the course of the 2010s were replaced by individual pickets and more symbolic events.[1] Stripping citizens of their civil rights and opportunities to participate in politics, the regime consistently employed repression strategies exemplifying authoritarian innovation. It increased risks associated with protests and successfully reduced the number of citizens willing to openly express their disagreement with the authorities. The regime dramatically reshaped contentious politics and participation in Russia.

But how exactly did the regime change the nature of contention? Existing literature suggests that repression may be one of the key factors in reducing contentious action, while it may also paradoxically facilitate contention (Lichbach, 1987; Moore, 1998; K.-D. Opp, 1994). Even regimes classified as highly repressive are still prone to contentious events and must address them to different degrees. In Russia, despite the regime's attempts to intimidate and imprison participants following 2011–2012, contentious action persisted throughout the 2010s. It is worth noting that, even before 2011, the Russian regime was infamous for suppressing contentious action through force and eliminating opponents without any significant effort to conceal it (Daucé, 2014; Politkovskaya, 2012; Robertson, 2013). None of this prevented contention, and there is no evidence suggesting that repression alone was the primary driver for this change in the way people make claims against the state.

Recent literature on authoritarianism also indicates that the development of such regimes is not solely reliant on the use of force (Guriev & Treisman, 2020; Morgenbesser, 2020a). Instead, a variety of strategies employed in authoritarianism brings up another significant aspect that academic literature on contentious action overlooks. It is the notion that authoritarian regimes are not exclusively rigid, and for their survival, they may employ a combination of methods to remain in power and prolong their monopoly on politics – or innovation (Curato & Fossati, 2020; Morgenbesser, 2020b). Depending on the challenges that threaten them, authoritarian regimes may utilize diverse tactics and strategies to exercise control, even if they initially appear as concessions or the onset of democratization. The ability to confront and address these challenges determines the regime's survival and, therefore, necessitates constant adaptation of its attributes, such as repression.

---

[1] The examples of such symbolic events include flower protests where people brought flowers to places with Ukrainian history, for example, monuments to prominent Ukrainians, as a display of solidarity with Ukraine after Russia's full-scale invasion of Ukraine in 2022 (Rossman, 2022). Anti-war and anti-regime graffiti, arsons of military recruitment centers, and replacing supermarket price labels are other examples.

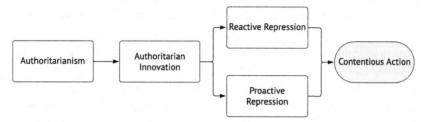

Figure 1 The relationship between authoritarianism and contention.

The use of authoritarian innovation is crucial to the regime in the context of contentious politics. For example, while the Russian regime successfully contained the events of 2011–2012, it did not stop the use of repression in the subsequent years and did not simply employ the same strategies to disperse claim-makers. Instead, it employed concurrent and successive measures that went beyond individuals' detention and political persecution. In an effort to prevent or at least control future contention, the regime gradually restricted various aspects of civil liberties using methods previously absent in Russian politics. Through changing specific elements of the political system, the regime gradually achieved its ends. The innovation encompassed a variety of strategies that evolved over time, introducing punishments for political participation, affiliation, actions, and, eventually, words published on social media or pronounced in private conversations. Together with the increase in violence, these measures enabled the regime to change how contention takes place, gaining more control over the range of issues that people make claims against and preventing more contentious events.

This Element explores how authoritarian regimes shape contention through innovation (Figure 1). The innovation here refers to repressive strategies employed by a political regime to infringe on civil liberties, thus changing contentious action and ensuring regime longevity. I analyze how authoritarian politics may either increase or decrease contention by violating democratic freedoms. The Element argues that innovation can be operationalized in terms of proactive and reactive repression, which refer to specific actions undertaken by the regime to deter citizens from participating in future contentious events or suppress ongoing contention. With this understanding of proactive and reactive forms of repression, I establish a causal link between them and contention. Specifically, I examine how innovative strategies may precipitate changes in contentious action and its repertoires. I then propose a theory that explains how a political regime may impact contention. Drawing upon authoritarian developments in Russia and its eighty-three federal subjects, I explore whether the authoritarian regime has increased or, on the contrary, decreased contention federally and regionally over the time frame from the State Duma elections in 2011 until March 2023, one year after Russia's full-scale invasion of Ukraine.[2]

This approach enables me to address several issues largely unexplored in contentious political literature. First, the proposed theoretical framework establishes the link between political regime and contention by defining continuous and subsequent infringements on civil liberties as the primary element that structures citizens' political participation and, therefore, contentious action. Second, I explore how actual individual policies and decisions may limit political participation. Instead of exploring regime classifications and their general attributes, I focus on specific strategies undertaken by a repressive rule over the 2011–2023 time frame. It allows me to take a closer look at how these strategies may lead to short- and long-term changes in the way people make claims against the state. Third, the Element explores the spatial and temporal distribution of contentious action. This examination of how regional contention changes geographically and over time in response to repressive strategies employed by the regime may shed more light on how contention is structured. Lastly, this research determines the role of always-evolving authoritarian institutions and policies in shaping contention. By analyzing the impact of consistent authoritarian innovation, this Element offers a novel theoretical framework for explaining how authoritarian regimes shape contention and how they can anticipate and preempt contentious actions.

The following section reviews existing scholarship that explores the relationship between authoritarian rule and contention. It highlights how previous studies have explored contentious actions in different political regimes and identifies gaps in our current understanding. Focusing on authoritarianism, this discussion moves toward the concept of repression, long considered one of the key determinants of contentious action. By drawing on literature discussing authoritarianism and repression, the concept of authoritarian innovation is introduced and conceptualized in the subsequent theoretical and empirical discussion of its relationship with contentious action.

---

[2] Federal subjects are administrative units in Russia, composed of oblasts, autonomous oblasts, autonomous districts, krais, republics, and cities of federal importance. The title of a federal subject does not change its legal status in its relationship with the federal government; all of them are equally represented in the Federation Council. However, federal subjects may vary in their government structure, the presence of elected executives, and the composition of their parliaments. Any territories annexed by Russia during the war in Ukraine in 2014 and from 2022 onward are not recognized as Russian and are not included in the analysis in this Element.

2 Explaining Authoritarianism and Contentious Action

An extensive body of literature analyzes the factors that contribute to contentious action within Western democracies, characterized by political pluralism, competition, and protection of civil rights (Chen & Moss, 2018; Ong & Han, 2019). Decades of research have yielded a multitude of theories and concepts focused on explaining contentious action, its underlying mechanisms, and the reasons for its varied prevalence across societies (K. Opp, 2022; K.-D. Opp, 2009). As Goldstone (2016, 117) points out, contentious action in democracies is a complementary form of political participation, serving as a "normal adjunct to political party competition." Contentious events are expected to draw attention to overlooked issues, thus prompting a state response to regain legitimacy among claim-makers (Goldstone, 2016, 107). Political opportunity structures (Eisinger, 1973; McAdam & Tarrow, 2018), individual motivations (Snow et al., 2018), and resource accessibility (J. D. McCarthy & Zald, 1977), along with various other theories (K.-D. Opp, 2009), have been utilized to explain contention across different contexts.

However, questions remained over whether this definition of contention and its contributing factors would change under conditions where freedoms such as speech and association are constrained, elections are not free and fair, censorship is ubiquitous, political persecution is commonplace, and the legal system lacks independence. Owing to an affinity – or perhaps unintentional bias – toward democracies in the field (Corduneanu-Huci & Osa, 2003; McAdam et al., 2012), there has been limited research on how specific characteristics unique to authoritarian regimes might shape contention in comparison to less restrictive systems on the democratic spectrum. While certain perspectives have been employed to explain the occurrence of individual instances of contentious action in authoritarian regimes, there is a need for a more comprehensive understanding of the fundamental processes leading to contention particularly when it comes to authoritarianism.[3] I begin addressing this gap by exploring and defining the specific attributes of political regimes that categorize them as authoritarian and linking them to the phenomenon of contentious action.

2.1 Participation and Contestation as Political Regime Attributes

Modern research and literature often categorize regime types based on a specific definition of democracy, with Dahl's (1971) definition of polyarchy,

---

[3] These include the political opportunity theory (e.g., contentious events in El Salvador from 1962–1981[Almeida, 2003] and the Philippines and Burma in the 1980s[Schock, 1999]) and resource mobilization theory (e.g., Tunisia in 2010–2011[Breuer et al., 2015]).

based on the attributes of participation (inclusion) and contestation, being the most popular choice. Dahl identified seven institutions crucial for democracy, including the presence of elected officials, free and fair elections, freedom of expression, access to alternative sources of information, freedom of association, inclusive citizenship, and the right of citizens to directly or indirectly participate in the government. These attributes are discussed in-depth in the literature. While there is a general agreement on the significance of these particular regime attributes, ongoing discussions about how they should be conceptualized, measured, and aggregated have led to a variety of categorizations, each with its own conceptualizations of democracy and operationalizations of their attributes (Munck & Verkuilen, 2002).

Regime classification providers use various measures and introduce unique categorizations to explain different categories along the democratic spectrum. Some prefer to focus on binary classifications, distinguishing between democracy and nondemocracy (Carles et al., 2018), while others utilize continuous measures based on numeric scores (Coppedge et al., 2016). To explain the variation within democratic and nondemocratic regime types, some publications have zeroed in on institutional arrangements (Anckar & Fredriksson, 2019; Bjørnskov & Rode, 2019). In contrast, others have emphasized the presence of contested elections (Lührmann et al., 2018) and the role of political parties and civil liberties (Magaloni et al., 2013; Skaaning, 2021). When assigning scores to operationalize regime types, scholars often prioritize specific attributes over others; some use broader maximalist definitions of democracy encompassing numerous attributes (Freedom House, 2023; Marshall et al., 2010), while others limit their focus to the presence and conduct of contested elections (Anckar & Fredriksson, 2019; Bjørnskov & Rode, 2019) or the status of civil liberties (Skaaning, 2021). The measures employed by classification providers affect how a political regime is categorized, impacting whether it is labeled as a democracy or nondemocracy and consequently influencing research findings.

Despite difficulties in determining which practices contribute more to authoritarianism or democracy or whether they should all be weighed equally, the degree to which the attributes of participation and contestation are violated determines the level of democracy or authoritarianism. However, the measures of participation and contestation are also problematic. For example, while most authoritarian regimes conduct elections with differing levels of competitiveness, how they incorporate these practices into their politics can be problematic to discern. The mere presence of elections does not necessarily indicate whether a regime is more democratic, especially in scenarios where other attributes do not provide access to the political system and opportunities to impact the political process. As Glasius (2018) suggests, while modern regime classifications often emphasize elections as necessary to identify a political regime type, their importance can be overestimated in regimes lacking other democratic attributes.

However, what differentiates authoritarian regimes from one another is their institutions that ensure and restrict citizen participation in politics, including contention. These regimes deploy a variety of strategies to achieve political outcomes, including surveillance (for example, digital surveillance as a tool for repression and co-optation in China [Xu, 2021]), discrimination against particular groups of people (as seen with identity politics in Indonesia [Mietzner, 2020]), and physical violence (exemplified by the violent suppression of contentious events in 2017–2019 in Iran [Shahi & Abdoh-Tabrizi, 2020]). Thus, authoritarianism is fundamentally determined by such policies and actions that violate civil liberties and create regimes where citizens' decision-making is minimized for the benefit of the rule. Therefore, the Element posits that authoritarianism is defined as the practices employed by political regimes to manipulate accessibility to the political system and restrict citizen participation and contestation – essentially, repression – that further impacts contentious politics.

The field of contentious politics has yet to engage with these advancements fully. Issues related to regime categorization and the impact of specific regime attributes on contention are often overlooked. The selection of attributes that classify a regime as authoritarian is seldom addressed in detail and is often speculative. Instead, a regime type is assumed to be authoritarian without thoroughly examining the attributes that render it so and how these characteristics may influence contentious action. The concept of authoritarianism is not clearly defined, even though different authoritarian regimes employ distinct strategies to retain power, maintain political institutions (Gandhi & Przeworski, 2007; Levitsky & Way, 2002), repress (Maddi et al., 2006), manipulate political opportunities (Osa & Schock, 2007), mobilize supporters, and respond to those making claims against the state (Goldstone & Tilly, 2001; Hellmeier & Weidmann, 2020; Meyer, 2004). Literature on contentious action in authoritarianism, which focuses on specific geographic areas, often needs a more systematic understanding of these differences and their broader impact on contentious politics. Nevertheless, developments in the fields of political regime classification and democratization (Alvarez et al., 1996; Bjørnskov & Rode, 2020; Przeworski et al., 2000), as well as the ever-changing practices of authoritarianism (Levitsky & Way, 2010; Schedler, 2013), make contributions to how the relationship between politics and contention is perceived. They enhance our understanding of how politics shape noninstitutional participation in contexts where contention is not merely a complementary resource for making claims against the state but also one of the few available and dangerously risky tools for effecting political change.

2.2 Defining Contentious Action

How contention or contentious action is defined varies across the scholarly literature.[4] In this Element, the definition is drawn from Straughn (2005) and S. Tarrow (2022). It is a joint effort individuals undertake to confront authorities in response to official actions or policies. The term repertoire of contention refers to a limited set of routines learned, shared, and performed through a relatively deliberate process of choice and emerge from interaction and experiences of contentious action (Tilly, 1993, 264). These routines are limited to familiar claim-making methods previously used within society. They are derived from past experiences, interactions, and observations rooted in cultural and historical contexts. While repertoires of contention evolve, and newer methods may supplant obsolete routines, such changes are gradual and are influenced by various factors, including interactions with the regime.

This Element classifies any effort to confront the regime in furtherance of particular interests as contention. While some forms of contention may be more likely to provoke repression or concessions (e.g., physical violence against law enforcement officers versus nonviolent rallies against low wages), contention is generally considered risky regardless of intent. What constitutes a threat is subject to variation across regimes and can change according to authorities' discretion (Ortmann, 2023). Thus, even though environmental and labor protests are often perceived as less likely to face repression (for example, the selective approach to suppressing contentious events in China [Göbel, 2021]), the assumption remains that repression can be used during any contentious event irrespective of its intent.

2.3 The Impact of Repression on Contentious Action

Much of the literature on contentious politics in authoritarianism revolves around repression as one of the main attributes that shape contention in such regimes. In his seminal work, Moore (1998) refers to a major debate on the role of repression in reducing and increasing contentious action. He argues

---

[4] Contentious action or contention is referred to by different scholars as protest (della Porta, 2011; K. Opp, 2022; K.-D. Opp, 2009; Van Stekelenburg et al., 2018), collective action, and dissent among others. Some definitions of contention and protest focus on particular attributes (e.g., Biggs [2015] focuses on the criterion of powerfulness, S. G. Tarrow [1989] prioritizes the component of disruption over violence. In contrast, Lipsky [1968] pays more attention to the component of reward, emphasizing the aim of claim-makers to obtain rewards from political and economic systems).

that repression may both deter and spark dissident behavior, and both of these claims may be substantiated. Moore's statistical analysis gives credence to the rational actor model by Lichbach (1987), who suggested that an escalation in governmental repression could suppress nonviolent contentious action but simultaneously incite violence. Another critical observation by Lichbach (1987) refers to consistency in repression: consistent accommodative and repressive policies reduce contention, while inconsistencies increase it.

Drawing from the findings presented by Lichbach (1987), Gupta et al. (1993) modify his theory and put an emphasis on the dynamics of the relationship between repression and contention. According to the study, the way repression impacts contentious action depends on the nature of the regime. They further elucidate that the type of political regime determines the impact of repression on contention. Gupta et al. (1993) note that repression's nature varies significantly between democracies and nondemocracies, representing two opposite political systems. While democracies find solutions within the political process, nondemocracies can impose severe repressions on claim-makers without regard for human rights and other constraints present in democracies. These repressions place unbearable costs on claim-makers, thus preventing them from engaging in contentious action (Gupta et al., 1993).

Existing definitions and classifications of repression vary in scope. The body of work from the past decade suggests that modern authoritarian regimes use a blend of different tactics and repertoires to repress. Being an essential attribute of authoritarianism, repression inherently pertains to the violation of civil liberties. The variance in the repertoire of repression methods across regimes is clear, with a common understanding that repression can differ in intensity, technology, and scope (targeted or random). Siegel (2011, 997) defines repression as removing individuals from a social network through methods such as execution, imprisonment, or rendition. Such strategies allow the regime to deter citizens from participating in contentious events. Exploring collective action in Mexico, Trejo (2012) categorizes repression as targeted, moderate, harsh, lethal, or nonlethal, depending on its strength, direction, and method. Similarly, Loveman (1998) examines collective action in Chile, Uruguay, and Argentina, categorizing repression based on its extent and intensity, and acknowledges the presence of "extralegal forms of repression" (Loveman, 1998, 509). However, Moss (2014, 262) critiques the focus on the relative severity of repression and its impact on the volume of contention, arguing that this perspective does not adequately explain contention within repressive environments.

Measuring repression is challenging in modern authoritarian regimes that prefer a variety of indirect methods and mimicry over overt violence. This issue is especially pertinent when repression refers not directly to the use of force but to a set of preemptive measures to achieve authoritarian ends. While the scope of repression can be quantified and measured by the number of instances of violence, political persecutions, and prisoners, it is problematic to measure repression when it is proactive or data availability is insufficient. A similar argument is presented by Moss (2014, 263), who refers to a body of literature on repression and contentious action, pointing out that softer techniques such as channeling, silencing, and surveillance effectively "attenuate activism." Drawing on a study of repression and collective action in Jordan, she concludes that these methods allow the regime to maintain a "veneer of liberalism" (Moss, 2014, 263) while undermining claim-makers, yet often remaining unaccounted for in traditional data sources, complicating their analysis.

Due to the increasing sophistication of strategies employed by authoritarian regimes to maintain longevity, understanding these methods becomes crucial. These regimes develop elaborate strategies to prevent citizen engagement in activities deemed potentially threatening, moving beyond direct repression to employ preventive measures (Tertytchnaya, 2023). For example, Ritter and Conrad (2016) highlight that the presence of dissent does not necessarily lead to direct repression, as regimes may opt for preemptive tactics instead. This approach forces regime opponents to self-censor in anticipation of a repressive response, thereby making them act more cautiously and decreasing threats to the regime.

Horvath (2011) focuses on how the threat of revolutions in Ukraine and Georgia spreading to Russia pressured the Kremlin to develop preventative strategies, such as increasing control over the NGO sector, creating the state-sponsored Nashi movement, and promoting the ideology labeled as sovereign democracy, portrayed as a response to foreign threats. These measures strengthened the regime's control over the opposition. In studying the impact of repression on public opinion, Tertytchnaya (2023) posits that preventative repression, such as requiring authorization before holding a rally, impacts the opposition's ability to garner the necessary support. It also allows the regime to increase the costs of participation and prevents the opposition from attracting more supporters. Additionally, Tertytchnaya (2023) notes that modern authoritarian regimes also use tactics that involve limited coercion against the opposition but implement restrictions and legislation to limit the rights of participation in rallies and other activities to specific groups of citizens. By using targeted forms of restrictions to prevent particular actors from engaging in contentious politics and investing efforts to discredit them in the eyes of the public, they aim to limit the growth of such groups.

Following these developments in the literature, this Element defines repression as restrictive measures employed by the regime to reduce access to participation and contestation, thereby preventing citizens from engaging in politics and making political claims that challenge the existing political structure or decision-making. Serving the regime's interests, repression infringes upon civil liberties. Building on Snyder's (1976) research, I distinguish between reactive and proactive (preventative) forms of repression. The use of these two subclasses helps to account for possible variations in repressive techniques. Reactive repression refers to measures the regime employs in response to specific ongoing contentious events, while proactive repression occurs preventatively in the absence of such activity. This approach allows for a temporal exploration of how the regime may combine repressive strategies over time to impact contentious action and how the regime's approach to participation may change over time. Table 1 offers examples from the literature delineating proactive and reactive repression to make this distinction clearer. Although this is not an exhaustive list of repressive strategies universally employed by authoritarian regimes, it provides a baseline classification of the regime's actions aimed at restricting participation before, during, and after contentious events.

2.4 From Authoritarian Learning to Innovation

As scholars have become increasingly attuned to variations in the repertoires of repression in authoritarian regimes, facilitating classification and distinctions among types of repression (Earl, 2011), attention has also grown toward how political regimes learn and choose new ways of repression and why particular strategies are adopted by some regimes but not others. While it is widely perceived that regimes repress and adopt different practices to remain in power in reaction to both objective or subjective threats (Davenport, 1995; Earl, 2003, 2011), the question of why or under what circumstances regimes deploy particular strategies and prefer certain repressive strategies over others has not been systematically explored. Addressing this gap, the concept of authoritarian learning has emerged, suggesting that authoritarian regimes may adopt survival strategies "based upon the prior successes and failures of other governments" (Hall & Ambrosio, 2017, 143). This notion gained traction, especially in light of increasing perceived threats to authoritarian regimes during the color revolutions in Georgia and Ukraine in the early 2000s and the Arab Spring in 2011 (Heydemann & Leenders, 2011). Observing revolutionary events in Ukrainie, Georgia, Tunisia, Egypt, and Libya led authoritarian regimes, including those in Russia, China, Saudi Arabia, and Algeria, to take preventative measures to maximize their survival chances. They deployed a variety of strategies, including violent repressions against regime opponents, focusing on increasing

Table 1 Examples of reactive and proactive repression strategies employed by authoritarian states

Type	Form	Definition	Examples
Reactive repression	Arrests and incarceration	Apprehensions to deter participation	Arrests in Azerbaijan (LaPorte, 2015) and China (Jay Chen, 2020)
	Physical violence	The use of physical force to disperse protests	Violence in Syria (Heydemann, 2013) and the use of live rounds in Hong Kong (Chau & Wan, 2024)
	Crowd control	Dispersing and dividing protests using aggressive crowd management	No-protest areas and blockading routes to specific locations in Malaysia (Boon, 2022)
	Digital tactics	Preventing communication among protesters	Blocked cellular services in Egypt (Hassanpour, 2014) and blocked access to internet in Myanmar (Van Laer & Van Aelst, 2013)
Proactive repression	Political persecution	Politically motivated legal action against individuals participating in protests	Charges against activists in Belarus (Ash, 2015) and Turkey (Esen & Gumuscu, 2016)
	Physical violence	The use of murder, torture, and other forms of physical harm against activists	Assassination of activists associated with particular protests and movements in Iraq (Mustafa, 2023)

Threats and intimidation	Using threats and intimidation tactics against individuals to deter participation	Intimidation in Sri Lanka (Adamson, 2020)
Surveillance	Covert strategies for sanctioning individuals or groups	Surveillance and arrests in China (Xu, 2021)
Repressive legislation	Legal restrictions placed in violation of civil liberties	Emergencies in Turkey (Arslanalp & Erkmen, 2020) and fines and imprisonment for criticism of the Russian army and government actors (L. A. McCarthy et al., 2023)
State censorship	Sanctions against dissenting views	State censorship in Russia (Gabdulhakov, 2020)
Pro-regime protest	Events arranged by pro-regime actors using coercion or incentives for participants	Pro-regime mobilization in Hong Kong (Yuen, 2023)

personal costs of participation (Heydemann & Leenders, 2011), and adopting each other's strategies deemed efficient to preempt increased contention, such as preemptive censorship and large-scale bans in Kazakhstan following the Chinese model of authoritarian stability (Hall & Ambrosio, 2017). The capacity to adapt to challenges by observing the examples of others has been interpreted as the authoritarian regime's ability to learn from both fellow authoritarian regimes and democracies (Heydemann & Leenders, 2014; Lang, 2018; Ortmann & Thompson, 2020).

However, evidence also suggests that in their process of authoritarian learning, regimes may often be guided by negative examples, not merely adopting policies deemed successful in other authoritarian contexts. Instead, they take preemptive steps to avoid similar pitfalls (Heydemann & Leenders, 2011; Lang, 2018). While it is true that authoritarian regimes engage with one another, the decision on which repressive strategies to borrow and implement is far from straightforward. It is a selective process, dependent on the unique challenges of each political regime (Lang, 2018). These challenges are shaped by the regime's unique attributes and the threats to its longevity. This complexity begets innovation, where regimes, influenced by both negative and positive examples, devise their own approaches to repression based on their specific circumstances and threats.

Indeed, relationships within the realm of contentious politics constantly evolve, necessitating that individuals challenging the regime innovate to overcome restrictions. McAdam (1983) emphasizes the dynamic of tactical interactions between the regime and claim-makers – individuals and groups positioned "outside of the polity" and confined to a state of "institutionalized political impotence" (McAdam, 1983, 735). To force the opponent to make concessions and ensure the enduring impact of their tactics, claim-makers may either integrate into institutionalized politics or seek noninstitutional forms to continue exerting pressure on institutionalized actors. Over time, even the most successful tactics may wane in effectiveness as the opponent adapts, thus requiring that protesters remain creative and devise new methods to address countermoves made by the regime.

In his work, McAdam (1983), referring to this process as tactical innovation, argued that the outcome of claims made by actors opposing the regime is significantly influenced by the latter's ability to counter innovative tactics. According to McAdam (1983), this interplay is embedded within specific sociohistorical contexts. Further expanding on this idea, Wang and Soule (2016), in their study of protests in the United States, pointed out that such innovations can emerge not only from tactics differing from the existing, routine ones but also from new "recombinations of familiar tactics" (Wang & Soule, 2016, 518).

Such tactical innovation in repertoires of contention can be shaped by external macrohistorical conditions and internal movement dynamics, and are efficient because of their disruptiveness, which may cause uncertainty, thus increasing chances of protesters to succeed (Taylor & Van Dyke, 2004).

However, the concept of tactical innovation has received limited attention in discussions about contentious action in authoritarian regimes. Much of the research has been directed toward democracies, such as the United States and Britain (Crossley, 2002; Edwards, 2016; Morris, 1984; Wang & Soule, 2016). While some studies suggest that tactical innovation is an important characteristic of contentious action in authoritarian regimes, for example, in Egypt (Boutros, 2017) or Tunisia (Yaghi, 2018), they do not tend to address how the difference in political regimes shapes this tactical innovation. Specifically, there is a lack of exploration into whether innovative responses and actions implemented by the opposition differ based on the regime's level of repressiveness and the constraints imposed on citizens (Shriver & Adams, 2010).

While citizens opposing the regime innovate in their claims against the regime, the question arises: Does the regime also innovate? Can this innovation occur independently, based on decisions and perceived threats, or is it part of the same tactical interaction? As contentious repertoires evolve, they present new challenges to political regimes. Just as innovation is initiated by regime opponents, and considering this is a tactical interaction (McAdam, 1983), it implies that the regime also innovates, in turn making claims and assertions against the opposition. Therefore, traditional methods previously used by the regime, such as repression, may become obsolete or not as effective in addressing threats posed by claim-makers.

Here is where the more recent concept of authoritarian innovation comes into play. This term refers to novel tactics authoritarian regimes use to suppress opposition. Curato and Fossati (2020, 1006) attribute suppressing the press, incarcerating opposition figures, spreading propaganda, promoting a culture of fear, co-opting opposition leaders, and nurturing loyalty through the cultivation of a personality cult, among other methods, as examples of such innovative responses. In their examination of this topic, Curato and Fossati (2020) describe authoritarian innovation as the adoption of nominally democratic institutions for authoritarian ends, with the innovation lying in the use of new tools of repression. As Pepinsky (2020, 1093) highlights, this concept allows scholars to move beyond conventional political regime classifications and to focus on "how political decisions constrain or open up the space for mass political participation." By deviating from the formal rules traditionally considered in the literature, the concept of authoritarian innovation explains how authoritarian regimes deploy repression to achieve their political objectives while also controlling and, when necessary, simulating political participation.

Furthermore, Pepinsky's (2020) definition, which suggests that innovation can constrain or open up space for participation, implies that innovation can be employed both as a response to specific actions and as an ad hoc application of tactics, depending on what the regime perceives as necessary for its longevity or to strengthen its rule, potentially preventing dissent even in the absence of a visible threat. This interpretation aligns with Moore's (1998) observation that repression can manifest in both reactive and proactive forms, with the former occurring during an ongoing instance of contention and the latter employed in the absence of visible dissent (Moore, 1998). In their conceptualization of authoritarian innovation, Curato and Fossati (2020) attribute the criterion of innovativeness to the specific context in which an innovative tool is introduced by the regime, regardless of whether it has been applied in other contexts, emphasizing that the novelty of this tool in the current regime setting is what matters.

2.5 Authoritarian Innovation and Contentious Action

In the literature, authoritarian innovation is depicted in two main forms. One form is as a specific action, such as "Fresh News" in Cambodia – an online news outlet used by the Cambodian regime, introduced alongside crackdowns on independent media (Norén-Nilsson, 2021), or the ROTC Cyber activity in Thailand for disseminating pro-military propaganda on social media (Wongngamdee, 2023). The other form is a long-term strategy that spans multiple areas. An example of this is the regime in Russia, where a combination of criminal prosecution and administrative violations serves as a set of tools for repression (L. A. McCarthy et al., 2023). Ford et al. (2021) argue that the way the Cambodian regime addressed the labor movement is not innovative in itself, as repressing labor movements is not a phenomenon unique to Cambodia. However, the innovation lay in the set of tactics used by the regime, which can be deemed innovative and helped the regime maintain a veneer of democracy for the international community while introducing repressive changes into labor governance (Ford et al., 2021).

A regime does not engage in repression at a consistent scale; rather, it adjusts its tactics in response to emerging challenges, shifts in internal political alignments, and the evolution of available repression tools. When seeking to enhance control, improve efficiency, address new threats, or adapt to internal changes, a regime adopts new methods of repression. This makes repression a dynamic attribute of the political system. Such adaptive combinations of repression strategies, employed to deter political participation, can be characterized as authoritarian innovation.

This definition aligns with the concept offered by Curato and Fossati (2020), who used the term within the context of authoritarian practices in Southeast Asia to describe contextual patterns of action that "produce or further entrench unaccountable exercises of power" (Curato & Fossati, 2020, 1007). Reframed within the specific context of contention and repression, it encapsulates actions designed to prevent citizens from engaging in politics and making claims against authoritarian regimes.

Each authoritarian regime crafts its strategies in contentious politics, utilizing various combinations of proactive and reactive repression. As Glasius (2018, 517) points out, these strategies include "the means of secrecy, disinformation, and disabling voice." While these innovations can diverge in terms of specific methods or "novel tools" of repression (Curato & Fossati, 2020, 1007), each regime employs distinct repertoires or authoritarian patterns – actions designed to maintain control over its citizens when it comes to political participation (Glasius, 2018). Consequently, authoritarian innovation can be characterized as a novel repertoire consisting of repression, both reactive and proactive, aimed at restricting political participation and contestation.

Summary: Explaining the Impact of Authoritarianism on Contention

No universally effective strategies exist for authoritarian regimes to control contention, and the impact of repression methods of contentious action varies widely. For example, using violence as a form of reactive repression can be conducive to more contention.[5]

As Grimm and Harders (2018) argue in a study of post-Arab Spring Egypt, contention persisted and transformed in its repertoires despite the violence against supporters of the ousted president after the military coup in 2013. This transformation demonstrated claim-makers' ability to adjust their strategies in response to the regime's violence. The claim-makers regrouped and altered their actions both spatially and temporally, introducing new forms such as human chains and hit-and-run events while transitioning from large-scale sit-ins to more creative tools in addition to marches. It allowed them to absorb the existing regime strategies and adjust their actions accordingly. The persistence of contention resulted in further authoritarian innovation, that is, the political

---

[5] Changes in contentious action are assessed based on a variety of metrics, including the number of participants, frequency of events, and repertoires – that is, actors, actions, sequences of events, or a combination thereof (Biggs, 2018; Kriesi et al., 2019).

persecution of key activists, assigning the Muslim Brotherhood the status of a terrorist organization, and the implementation of relevant laws that criminalized protests. By 2017, the frequency and scale of contention were reduced considerably, which, according to Grimm and Harders (2018, 14), was a long-term result of repression. This example demonstrates that the use of diverse repression strategies results in varied outcomes. Through authoritarian innovation, contention can be reduced to a level where it no longer poses a threat, leading to reductions in both frequency and intensity.

How do authoritarian regimes shape contention? This Element emphasizes the importance of innovation, specifically the regime's ability to introduce new repressive strategies aimed at preventing claims against the regime. I argue that given the complex and dynamic nature of contention and political participation, regimes must adopt dynamic measures to effectively manage and contain dissent. Failure to address the changing dynamics of contentious action beyond traditional repertoires will leave a regime incapable of maintaining control over contention, leading to increased participation and evolving forms of protest.

Large-scale contentious events in Russia during the State Duma and the presidential election were unprecedented in their size, including the number of events and the diversity of participants. They maintained quality attributes or repertoires that had been developing over the previous decade when thousands of events took place all over the country (Lankina, 2015; Robertson, 2013). Lankina (2015) argues that repression had been used against rally participants prior to 2008, thus potentially shaping contention as well as its repertoires. Liberalization with the reduction in the use of repression against regime opposition in the period of Dmitry Medvedev's presidency (2008–2012) contributed to contentious action and may have been conducive to the 2011–2012 events. The reassumption of power by Vladimir Putin in 2012 marked an increase in repression (Lankina, 2015): arrests, intimidation, and political persecution, and employment of a wide range of strategies, including surveillance and channeling. While these efforts did not eliminate contention, they introduced an ongoing impact on contention's quantity and quality attributes, gradually restructuring contentious politics and using various strategies to contain and transform contention and its repertoires.

This Element also argues that innovation refers to both concurrent and successive introduction of proactive and reactive repression strategies. Within the confines of authoritarianism as a characteristic of a political system, the regime exerts control over political participation and contestation, thereby preventing citizens' active involvement in the political discourse. Innovation can be applied to repress an ongoing contentious event (e.g., the use of new crowd dispersal techniques) as well as to prevent a past event from occurring (e.g., the introduction of new legislation regulating rallies). Concurrent and successive use of repressive strategies previously unknown in contentious politics of the regime decreases contention because it makes the existing repertoires of contention obsolete, deterring citizens from claim-making due to possible unknown implications of innovation and the need to adapt the existing repertoires of contentious action and qualitative attributes to ensure further participation. If the regime continues to engage in contentious politics by dynamically introducing authoritarian innovation, it will negatively impact participation and contentious action in the long run. Any change in repertoires of contention takes time, and consistent authoritarian innovation impacts the process of changes in contention.[6] The regime's ability to innovate dynamically, adapting its repression strategies in response to the ever-evolving landscape of political contention, is a decisive factor in its control over the repertoires of contention and its longevity.

This section has outlined key attributes and concepts from the existing literature on authoritarian politics and contentious action, defined the fundamental attributes of authoritarianism, and offered a theoretical framework for understanding how authoritarian regimes shape contentious action through innovative proactive and reactive repression strategies, drawing from their own experiences and those observed in other regimes. The next section will describe the methodology employed in the empirical portion of this analysis.

3 Methodology

3.1 Russia as a Case Study

Modern authoritarianism in Russia is characterized by its strategies employed to restrict civil liberties and citizen participation in politics. What distinguishes Russia further is its simultaneous transformation of contention after the 2011–2012 parliamentary and presidential elections. In response, the regime deployed proactive and reactive repressive strategies such as law enforcement, violence against detainees and event participants, intimidation, political persecution, surveillance, and channeling methods as tools to restrict freedoms and affect resource flow and event occurrence. This innovation noticeably impacted contentious action, changing it step-by-step over the following decade.

Russia's authoritarian innovation was phased, introducing proactive and reactive repressive strategies in stages. The 2012–2015 period saw an increase

---

[6] As Tilly (2010, 35) argues, "repertoires vary from place to place, time to time, and pair to pair," innovating within established limits for "their place, time, and pair." S. Tarrow (1993, 283) points out that repertoires change "very slowly, constrained by overarching configurations of economics and state-building, and by the slow pace of cultural change."

in proactive repression and a surge in legislative changes as steps to restrict the existing civil liberties and access to politics. Between 2016 and 2019, the focus shifted toward constitutional and structural changes, such as the introduction of more repressive laws allowing the regime to employ state-wide control over the spread of information in the media and on the internet. In 2020–2023, the regime concluded its transformation with a surge in restrictive laws designed to prevent citizens from making a wide range of claims. The study explores this process, providing a comprehensive account of authoritarianism and how it impacted contentious action.

Russia presents a compelling case due to the diverse authoritarian configurations that coexist within a single regime. Although it has a de facto centralized structure, with its eighty-three federal subjects heavily dependent on the federal center (Nicholson, 2020), notable regional variations exist. These include differences in political structures and elections, levels of support for the president and the ruling party, governance styles, degrees of repressiveness, and overall relationships with the federal government. Such variations might lead to differences in contention, even though these regions are part of a singular authoritarian regime. This Element examines some of these regional differences.

3.2 Contentious Events Data

Data on contentious events in authoritarian regimes are often scarce and subject to inherent biases, resulting from underreporting, false reporting, censorship (including self-censorship), and limited access (Dollbaum, 2021a). Lankina (2015) overcame this obstacle by accessing data published by human rights activists reporting from various locations in Russia. Zhang and Pan (2019) employed machine learning techniques to extract information on contentious events posted by Weibo users in China. Obtaining reliable data depends on specific measures taken by the regime to restrict access to information and the presence of organizations, individual activists, and observers who have knowledge of or attend contentious events. While relevant publications related to contention tend to exist, the data are rarely systematic and not presented consistently.

3.2.1 Twitter (X) Protest Reports

Figure 2 illustrates the workflow to gather and generate the dataset on contentious events in Russia. The dataset utilizes social media posts by users on Twitter from January 2010 to March 2023 to account for the 2011–2023 time frame and the preceding year. While Dollbaum (2021b) notes that the use of

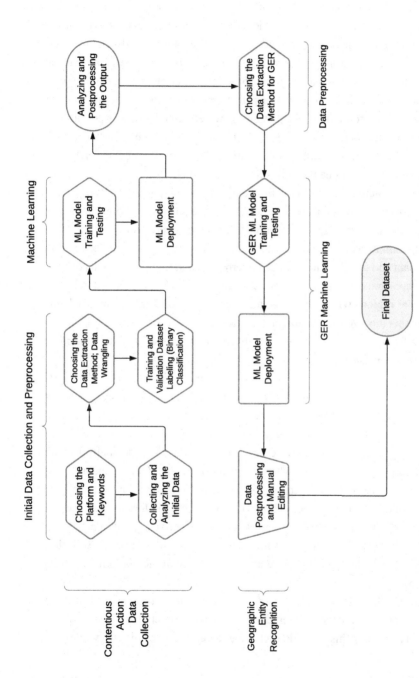

Figure 2 Methodological workflow for contentious events data collection in Russia.
Note: GER stands for Geographic Entity Recognition.

Twitter in Russia is considerably lower compared to the more popular social network, VK, especially outside of Moscow and Saint Petersburg, Twitter remains a key platform for opposition activists and politicians to communicate with their audiences (Alieva et al., 2022; Dollbaum, 2021b) and overseas users, for example, English speakers or Russians living overseas. Alexanyan et al. (2012) argue that Twitter users form distinct clusters and maintain user communities within Russian regions, fostering more consistent engagement and community formation. The platform is widely used to discuss politics and contentious events (Alexanyan et al., 2012), and as a medium for "discursive struggles" between the state and opposition in restrictive contexts, such as in Iran and Russia (Dehghan & Glazunova, 2021, 743).

Twitter, functioning as a network of activists, encompasses media organizations operating both online and offline, as well as exclusively Twitter, alongside individual users who report and publish firsthand observations, such as their participation in contentious events. It makes Twitter a valuable source of additional data and details that might be underreported in traditional media outlets. Underreporting could occur for various reasons, including protests taking place in remote regions with scarce media presence or intentional media blackouts during specific events. Leveraging Twitter facilitates access to a wide array of data from diverse media sources, offering unique insights from individual activists and eyewitnesses.

The choice of Twitter was also guided by more practical considerations. There are serious limitations related to the use of other platforms in Russia. For example, there is evidence that content on VK, one of the most popular Russian social networks, is censored, and its users are more frequently repressed for posting content (Bodrunova et al., 2021; Pan, 2017), potentially leading to self-censorship and biases when reporting on events. Other popular social media platforms, such as Facebook, YouTube, and Telegram, can potentially be sources of data on contentious action. However, these platforms restrict access to their API and impose other limitations on the collection of public data, which may negatively impact data availability and the quality of the dataset. Such limitations include the type of content and the usability of the platforms by users who post it.[7]

Figure 3 illustrates the diversity of actors reporting on contentious events on Twitter, derived from users' interactions with protest-related tweets included in the final dataset. In this network, each node represents a Twitter user, while each

---

[7] Despite this, using data from other social networks and understanding their limitations in collecting data for protest event analysis in Russia warrant further discussion, which falls outside the scope of this Element.

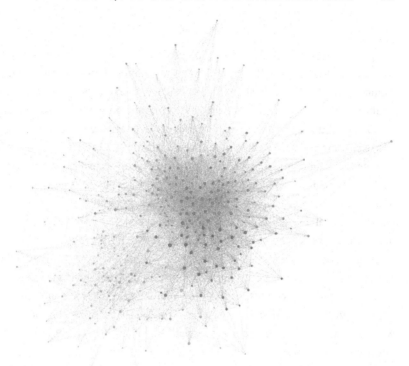

Figure 3 Network of influential users based on interactions with tweets from the dataset, including anti-regime bloggers and activists (●) pro-regime media (◉), satirical and entertainment anti-regime media (◉), anti-regime opposition actors (●) and CPRF (◉).
Note: The network, a directed bipartite graph, initially comprised 243,226 nodes and 960,875 edges. It was filtered based on an in-degree threshold of 450 interactions, resulting in a network of 362 nodes and 6,965 edges. The nodes represent two distinct categories: influential users and users interacting with these influentials via reposts, replies, or quotes.

directed edge signifies interactions (retweet, reply, or quote) with the posts of influential users who reported on protests from 2011 to 2023. The contributions of these users were crucial in creating the final protest dataset, demonstrating how other Twitter users engaged with the authors of the original tweets. Retweets and similar forms of interaction are regarded as reliable indicators of a user's influence within social networks (Cha et al., 2010; Riquelme & González-Cantergiani, 2016). Although this is not an exhaustive network of users who posted about protest events, it highlights the central users in disseminating protest information and enables the identification of which Twitter users were most notable in doing so. The accounts of influential users were classified based on a manual assessment of their accounts.

3.2.2 Data Collection

The primary goal of this data collection process is to identify posts detailing contentious events across Russia. The main selection criterion is that the posts should provide information about the event's date, location, repertoire, and the number of attendees. Such posts are either from media outlets or individuals who attended these events, reported on the occurrences there, claimed to witness what appeared to be a contentious event, or shared others' observations and comments. Notably, the most significant events receive coverage from multiple Twitter accounts, each offering varying levels of detail. In contrast, smaller regional events usually have coverage from fewer accounts.[8]

For the initial data collection, 5,713,892 tweets, including retweets containing the words "rally" and "protest," were collected.[9] These results encompassed tweets discussing any topic using these two keywords. For example, it included references to contentious events abroad or unrelated issues, such as casual meetups or family disagreements. In order to streamline the dataset, empty tweets, reposts, and tweets composed of just one word were excluded. Furthermore, tweets not specifically referencing instances of contentious action or not providing event and location details were labeled for further removal. Given the vast volume of tweets, machine learning was chosen as a more efficient solution than manual labeling due to time and resource considerations.

3.2.3 Binary Classification Using RuBERT

The approach entailed a binary classification of tweets. Those tweets that provided information about a geographic location, specific sites in Russian cities or regions, the number of detentions, participants, overarching event features, or discussions were tagged as "1." Conversely, tweets with content deemed irrelevant or ambiguous were marked as "0." To solve this binary classification problem, I used a pre-trained Bidirectional Encoder Representations from Transformers (BERT) Natural Language Processing (NLP) model (Devlin et al., 2018). This open-source, state-of-the-art language model, developed by Google, is efficient at classification tasks that demand a contextual grasp of the content to assign an appropriate classifier (Mapes et al., 2019). Being

---

[8] Relying on users' accounts of contentious events may yield a broad range of events. However, some posts might not give adequate details, particularly for smaller events. Estimates regarding attendee numbers and event characteristics might be subjective and inaccurate. During periods of frequent contention in similar locations, distinguishing between reports on the same event versus different ones can be challenging, leading to overreporting.

[9] Data collection was conducted using the Academic Access to the Twitter Application Programming Interface (API) v2, prior to when it was fully deprecated in June 2023.

open-source, BERT offers flexibility in fine-tuning its parameters to enhance performance and requires fewer computational resources for classification.

Given that the dataset is in Russian, I fine-tuned a Russian model based on DeepPavlov's pre-trained BERT variant, RuBERT (Burtsev et al., 2018; Kuratov & Arkhipov, 2019). For training, I labeled 10,000 tweets, randomly sampled from between 2010 and 2023 (Grießhaber et al., 2020).[10] Fine-tuning of the model's parameters was conducted until achieving optimal performance on the validation dataset and an optimal F1 score on the test dataset.[11]

3.2.4 Geographic Entity Recognition

To pinpoint the geographic references within tweets, the OpenAI GPT-3.5 model was deployed. This output underwent manual refinement and leveraged Google's Geocoding API to determine the exact positions (i.e., latitude and longitude) of specified cities and federal subjects mentioned in the tweets. Duplicate entries that pertained to the same event but varied in event-related information (e.g., adjustments in repertoire, numbers, and location) were amalgamated. The remaining semantic duplicates were discarded by evaluating the cosine similarity of at least 80 percent. The comparison is based on sentence embeddings generated via RuBERT (Kuratov & Arkhipov, 2019; Reimers & Gurevych, 2019). Tweets devoid of details related to the place, location, and nature of contentious activities were also excluded.

This data collection process resulted in a final dataset of 66,935 reports that span across all federal subjects over 2010–2023 (March). To protect the identities of the tweet authors, the content associated with tweets was translated and succinctly summarized utilizing GPT-3.5 and Google's Translation API. The data related to identifying the original posts (post and author ID) were removed.[12] Table 2 demonstrates several examples drawn from this dataset.

---

[10] The labeling task leveraged OpenAI's GPT-4 model (Sainz & Rigau, 2021) to facilitate faster labeling by a single coder. Due to potential accuracy and performance issues inherent in using generative transformer models, I ensured the integrity of the gold-standard labels by manually verifying and adjusting the training dataset.

[11] The F1 score, a harmonic mean of the model's precision and recall, was 0.91 for irrelevant posts and 0.80 for relevant ones, with a weighted average of 0.88. The training process spanned sixty-one epochs, each consisting of sixty-four samples, and utilized a learning rate of 1e-3. The model incorporated three hidden layers and employed the AdamW optimizer (Loshchilov & Hutter, 2017).

[12] When dealing with contentious events data in authoritarian regimes, there are heightened security concerns due to state surveillance and the intrinsic risks that come with sharing information. Omitting any data that might inadvertently expose an author's identity is crucial. These potential hazards are mitigated by summarizing, employing machine translation, and eliminating any trace of personal information.

Table 2 Examples of events presented in the 2010–March 2023 contentious dataset for eighty-three Russian regions

Created at	Region	City	Exact place	Summary
Mar 3, 2021	Moscow	Moscow	Trinity Forest	The Moscow city branch of the LDPR party held solitary pickets to protest and show support for the preservation of the Troitsky Forest
Sep 6, 2017	Ivanovo Oblast	Ivanovo	Children of war	The administration of the city of Ivanovo, affiliated with the Communist Party of the Russian Federation (KPRF), will hold a meeting with the Children of War and the SU155 cooperative members
Feb 6, 2020	Vladimir Oblast	Vladimir	Lenin Square	On February 15 at 14:00, a sanctioned rally will take place on Lenin Square in Vladimir, dedicated to the unsuccessful launch of the waste reform in the regional center
Feb 24, 2012	Moscow	Moscow	Lubyanka	The Moscow City Hall has allowed the "Young Russia" movement to hold a rally on Lubyanka on March 5.

3.2.5 Paired Comparison and Cluster Analysis

To examine how contentious action compares across different federal subjects and find the most similar and different regions, I conducted a paired comparison. The analysis observed longitudinal changes in contention trends across regions. Given that some regions are significantly more populous than others and may, therefore, demonstrate variations in the number of contentious events, the focus was solely on trends illustrating how event occurrences evolved over time. The underlying assumption is that if contention trends shift similarly across regions, these changes might be influenced by authoritarian innovation.

Due to variations in event counts across different regions and times, these counts were normalized.[13] This normalization ensured that the absolute magnitudes of the event counts did not influence trend comparisons, allowing for a focus solely on shifts in trends over time. The equation for normalization is

$$X'_{i,j} = \frac{X_{i,j} - \mu_j}{\sigma_j}, \tag{1}$$

where $X_{i,j}$ represents the number of events in region j at time i. Here, μ_j denotes the mean of the number of events for region j across all time points, while σ_j signifies the standard deviation of the number of events for region j across all time points (months and years):

$$\mu_j = \frac{1}{N} \sum_{i=1}^{N} X_{i,j}, \tag{2}$$

$$\sigma_j = \sqrt{\frac{1}{N} \sum_{i=1}^{N} (X_{i,j} - \mu_j)^2}, \tag{3}$$

where σ_j represents the spread of the numbers around μ_j. N denotes the total number of data points for each region's time series – specifically, 159 months from the dataset, spanning from January 2010 to March 2023.

After the normalization process, the standardized values or trends $X_{i,j}$ for each region and time point were compared in pairs using the Euclidean distance.[14] The Euclidean distance acts as a metric to quantify the differences between regions' trends. In this context, a smaller Euclidean distance between two regions indicates more similar trends, while a larger distance suggests greater dissimilarity. The distance is calculated as follows:

---

[13] Normalization was achieved using the StandardScaler() function from the sklearn Python library (Buitinck et al., 2013).

[14] The pairwise Euclidean distances among all regions were computed using the pdist() function from the scipy.spatial.distance package in the Scipy library.

$$d(p,q) = \sqrt{(p1 - q1)^2 + (p2 - q2)^2 + \ldots + (pn - qn)^2}. \qquad (4)$$

The Euclidean distance is subsequently used for hierarchical clustering. In this approach, the two entities (either individual data points or existing clusters) with the shortest distance between them are merged. This process is repeated iteratively until all entities are merged into a single overarching cluster.[15] Figure 4 illustrates the hierarchy of the clusters in a dendrogram. The height at which two clusters merge in the dendrogram represents the degree of their dissimilarity: the higher the merging point, the greater the dissimilarity. The colors and merging heights delineate distinct clusters of regions with the most similarity.

In total, eight clusters were identified for further qualitative analysis using existing regional data on reactive and proactive repression forms, as well as reports on contention, to discern their similarities and differences. The list of clusters is shown in Table 3.

3.3 Repression Dataset

Data on reactive and proactive forms of repression were collected from several sources depending on the strategy of repression employed by the regime over the time frame from January 2010 to March 2023. To identify what innovative methods the regime introduced over the time frame to reduce access to participation and contestation, I focused on how new repressive legislation was introduced and what changes were made in regulating people's access to politics. I used data on political persecution to trace how activists engaged in politics were persecuted and what instruments the regime used against them.

Additional details regarding the officials' approval of specific contentious events, as well as actions taken by both the regime and claim-makers during periods of heightened contention, were sourced from the contentious events dataset. Approvals for major events were often reported on social media and opposition or news websites. Furthermore, data were gleaned from various open sources, including state-sponsored and opposition media and Russian and foreign news outlets (Table 4).

3.3.1 Repressive Legislation

Legislation is considered repressive if it violates fundamental human rights or can be potentially used to infringe on civil liberties of citizens. The

---

[15] Hierarchical clustering is performed using the linkage() function from the cluster.hierarchy package in the Scipy library.

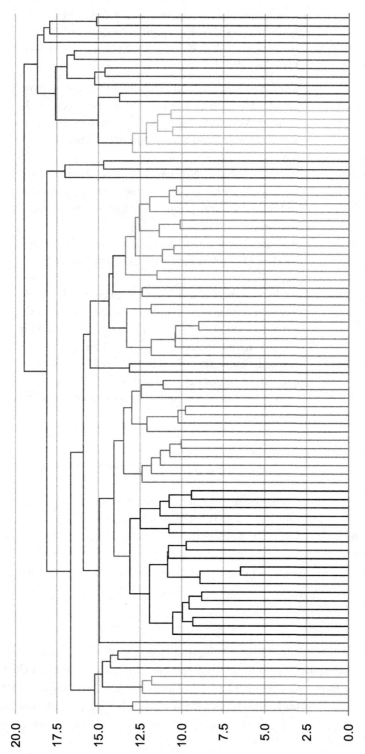

Figure 4 Clusters of similar and dissimilar regions in terms of contentious trends based on Euclidean distance.

Table 3 Regional clusters demonstrating contentious trend
similarities based on Euclidean distance

Cluster	Federal subject
Cluster 1	Kaliningrad, Kirov, Leningrad, Lipetsk, Nizhny Novgorod, Omsk, Rostov, Ryazan, Saratov, Sverdlovsk, Tyumen, Voronezh, Yaroslavl, and Volgograd Oblasts; Krasnodar and Perm Krais; Moscow and Saint Petersburg
Cluster 2	Irkutsk, Kaluga, Novgorod, Pskov, Samara, and Ulyanovsk Oblasts; Altai, Krasnoyarsk, Primorsky, and Stavropol Krais; Chuvashia, Mari El, and Udmurt Republics
Cluster 3	Arkhangelsk, Ivanovo, Kurgan, Moscow, Penza, and Tambov Oblasts; Dagestan, Khakassia, and Tatarstan Republics
Cluster 4	Bashkortostan, Kabardino-Balkarian, and Komi Republics; Belgorod, Kemerovo, Kursk, Novosibirsk, Orenburg, Oryol, Tomsk, Tver, Vologda, and Vladimir Oblasts; Khanty-Mansi Autonomous Okrug
Cluster 5	Adygea, Buryatia, Karachay-Cherkessia, Karelia, and Sakha Republics; Yamalo-Nenets Autonomous Okrug; Jewish Autonomous and Kostroma Oblasts; Zabaykalsky Krai
Cluster 6	Astrakhan and Magadan Oblasts; Chukotka and Nenets Autonomous Okrugs; North Ossetia-Alania, and Kalmykia Republics; Kamchatka and Khabarovsk Krais
Cluster 7	Amur, Bryansk, Chelyabinsk, Murmansk, Sakhalin, Smolensk, and Tula Oblasts; Mordovia Republic
Cluster 8	Chechen, Ingushetia, and Tyva Republics

Note: Clusters are located next to each other and identified based on the
merging height.

determination of whether a specific legislative act is repressive is carried out
by international and human rights organizations, such as the European Commission for Democracy through Law (the Venice Commission) and the International Federation for Human Rights. Repressive legislation can influence the
rights of certain social groups to voice their opinions (Venice Commission,
2013).

Table 4 Data sources used in this Element

Type	Aspect of data	Sources
Proactive repression reports	Repressive legislation	Administrative Code of Russia (Federal Assembly of the Russian Federation, 2023a), Criminal Code of Russia (Federal Assembly of the Russian Federation, 2023c), Federal Protective Service of the Russian Federation (2023), Yabloko (2021), FIDH (2018, 2023), Venice Commission (2021)
	Political persecution	OVD-Info (2023a)
Reactive Repression reports	Detentions	Judicial Department of the Supreme Court (2023); OVD-Info (2023b)
General narrative and individual instances of repression	State responses, individual instances of contention and persecution, instances of violence and injuries	Contentious event dataset and media reports, including pro-government, opposition and foreign media outlets, official publications, and news on instances of contention as well as repression (e.g., BBC, Deutsche Welle, RIA News, Interfax, OVD-Info, Meduza, Novaya Gazeta, Kommersant, RBC)

Legislative acts passed by the parliament and signed by the president are publicly published by the Russian government. Reports classifying repressive legislation published by human rights organizations and media were consulted to determine whether a specific legislative act could be deemed repressive. Changes in punishments for violation of regulations related to political participation are documented in the Code of Administrative Violations and the Criminal Code of the Russian Federation and were included in the analysis.

3.3.2 Detention during Contentious Events

Individuals detained for participating in contentious events in Russia are most commonly convicted under Article 20.2 of the Code of Administrative Offences and typically receive a warning or a fine. Law enforcement officers predominantly invoke this code for most detainees unless the participant committed additional offenses (e.g., an alleged assault on an officer, consumption or possession of drugs or alcohol, verbal attacks against specific social groups or the state). Detentions under violation of Article 20.2 are documented by the Judicial Department of the Supreme Court (Federal Assembly of the Russian Federation, 2022). In some cases, detentions are marked by instances of violence and torture, as reported by the media, human rights organizations, lawyers, and relatives of the detainees.

This Element categorizes the act of detention and violence against participants during the contentious event as reactive repression. Meanwhile, any actions taken post-detention are considered proactive, aiming to deter future participation by specific individuals or groups in contentious events.

3.3.3 Political Persecution

The definition of political persecution encompasses the deprivation of personal liberty and detention that violates international human rights conventions, such as the European Convention on Human Rights. This includes detentions for political reasons without evidence, or where evidence is fabricated, discriminatory detentions, and detentions that breach legal proceedings (Parliamentary Assembly, 2012). Typically, reports on these issues are compiled by human rights organizations, such as OVD-Info (2023a), Sova (2022), and Centre (2013). This Element uses the database of political persecution cases from OVD-Info, which combines data from multiple sources, including their direct work with political prisoners and reports from other organizations and experts.[16]

Based on these data, reports of contentious events generated by users, changes in legislation, politically motivated persecutions, detainees, and violence, I proceed further by tracing how repression and innovative responses changed contention within the time frame of 2011–2023.

4 Authoritarian Innovation and Contentious Action in Russia

This section introduces the repressive strategies employed by the regime prior to the contentious events of 2011–2012. Drawing from the contentious events dataset, publications by both pro-government and opposition media outlets,

---

[16] OVD-Info is an independent human rights media organization dedicated to advocating for human rights and ending political persecution in Russia.

and additional human rights organization reports, the section then narrates how repression and contention in Russia developed over the following decade.

The time frame is divided into three distinct periods: 2011–2015, 2016–2020, and 2021–2023. These periods are distinguished by the innovation adopted by the regime and how it impacted contention. I also examine individual, prominent instances of repression to illustrate the evolution of repression and the dynamics as authoritarianism advanced. I then delineate the regional trends of contentious action and summarize the developments within each of these periods.

4.1 Repression in the 2000s: Background

In the 2000s, the regime employed a multitude of measures against its most prominent critics, encompassing targeted political harassment, persecution, and even the murder of journalists, lawyers, and opposition members (Lipman, 2010; Roudakova, 2009).[17] While instances of repression were observed nationwide, some regions – especially the North Caucasus republics – witnessed a higher frequency of repression. Reports from these regions often included deaths, torture, abductions, imprisonments, and intimidation of regime critics (Human Rights Watch, 2008).

The 2000s saw relatively reduced levels of repression compared to other periods (Gel'man, 2016). Until 2012, the regime refrained from enacting laws specifically designed to target political opposition and limit civil liberties. However, remnants of the USSR's legal system, such as the ambiguous Law on Security with its broad definitions of terms like "security," "interests," and "threat," lingered within the Russian legislative system. This vagueness opened the door for subjective interpretation of what can be perceived as threats to state security. Moreover, the entities responsible for maintaining state security were not defined, granting the regime considerate discretion in this regard (Waller, 1993).

Therefore, the regime frequently turned to anti-extremist and anti-terrorist laws for judicial persecution. Articles 280 and 282 of the Criminal Code were used to target political activists and critics. As pointed out by human rights organizations, these articles were convenient to use due to their politicized nature; they contained ideological verbiage that could categorize opposition

---

[17] Examples include the murder of Larisa Yudina in the Kalmykia Republic in 1998, Maksim Maksimov in Saint Petersburg in 2004, Anna Politkovskaya in Moscow in October 2006, Farid Babaev in Dagestan in 2007, and Natalya Estimirova in Grozny in 2009 (Azhgikhina, 2007; Human Rights Watch, 2008; Smith, 2011).

activism and anti-regime actions as acts of extremism or terrorism (OVD-Info, 2014; SoVA Center, 2013).

  Reactive repression involved the detention of prominent activists during contentious events, the use of physical force against them, and limitations on venues where such events could take place. Article 20.2, introduced in 2001, emerged as the primary instrument against participants in these events. The data concerning detentions were first released in 2004, concurrent with the law that governs participation in contentious events (Federal Assembly of the Russian Federation, 2004; Federal Assembly of the Russian Federation, 2023b). This legislation outlines the process for obtaining preliminary approvals for mass events, encompassing rallies, pickets, and demonstrations.[18] From 2004 to 2010, the number of detainees and those convicted for participating in contentious events remained relatively stable despite notable spikes in such events throughout the 2000s.

  Overall, the Russian regime employed the same range of tools against its opponents throughout the 2000s. While detentions and violence did occur, police interference and direct repression were generally less frequent, with only around 20 percent of events seeing police intervention (Omelicheva, 2021).

4.2 The Crazy Printer of 2011–2015

This period is distinct due to a large number of changes that occurred in both contentious action and repression. The rallies of 2011–2012 were some of the largest in modern Russia's history, with a variety of opposition actors making claims against the fraudulent elections and politics of the government (Figure 5). The rallies resulted in repression followed by a long series of new strategies that the regime employed to prevent the occurrence of similar contentious events in the future. Due to the number of repressive laws enacted during the 2012–2015 period, the State Duma of that convocation became colloquially known as the Crazy Printer (Libman, 2017). By imprisoning and persecuting organizers and participants of the 2012 rallies and introducing new legislation, the regime began to change the way people participate in politics and make political claims.

  In 2011, contentious action took place around the country, with the largest number of events in Moscow and Saint Petersburg. Most of these events were state-authorized, nonviolent rallies focused on specific issues. Participants made claims against election fraud, corruption, environmental concerns like the

---

[18] In order to arrange a mass event, Russian law requires a preliminary application that needs to be approved by the officials. The application lists organizers, participants with an approximate number of attendees, a proposed location, activities to be held, and the duration.

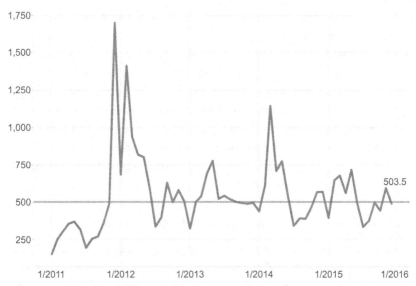

Figure 5 The state-wide number of reports on contentious events in
2011–2015.
Note: The horizontal line represents the average number of contentious events held
monthly around the country.

defense of Khimki forest, social issues including LGBTQ+ parades, as well as
labor conditions and delayed salaries. Additionally, supporters of political parties like the Liberal Democratic Party of Russia (LDPR) and the Communist
Party of the Russian Federation (CPRF) rallied, while others gathered to commemorate significant historical events and figures, such as victims of World
War II. This range of events was an ordinary part of Russia's contentious repertoires. However, unauthorized events sometimes faced dispersion, particularly
those critical of the regime's politics and United Russia – the ruling party
with a constitutional majority. Examples include the rallies at Triumph Square
and Chistoprudny Boulevard in April 2011. Larger demonstrations often had a
significant police and internal military presence, including units like OMON.[19]

   A significant change in the incidence and the number of participants occurred
after the State Duma election in December 2011. Contentious events surged
as the participants claimed that the election was fraudulent. Across the country, over 100,000 people participated in a series of events. In Moscow alone,
tens of thousands rallied, demanding election transparency and official resigna-
tions such as the resignation of the head of the Central Electoral Commission
and Vladimir Putin. Institutional and noninstitutional opposition actors were

---

[19] OMON is a special internal military force primarily acting as riot police.

present, including the Communist Party of Russia, A Just Russia, Pussy Riot, White Ribbon and Red Ribbon movements, Front for Change, Yabloko, Solidarity, PARNAS, and other independent bloggers, activists, and celebrities. Despite confrontations with police officers and an overall increase in detentions for participation in unsanctioned events and misconduct during mass events as per Article 20.2, physical violence did not happen. Moscow was the epicenter where the majority rallied, with major contentious events on December 5, 10, and 24. To attract more attention, the participants utilized media, the internet, and posters. Although the officials occasionally rescheduled or relocated events, they generally permitted them.

4.2.1 2012: the Presidential Election and the Bolotnaya Case

The events persisted into early 2012, especially in Moscow and Saint Petersburg. One of the most notable ones in terms of the number of participants took place on Vorobyovy Gory; there was an anti-fascist event on the January 19th and a rally for fair elections on the January 21st. Simultaneously, some environmental (e.g., in defense of the Bitsevsky forest) and commemorative (e.g., in memory of Stanislav Markelov and Anastasia Baburova) events took place.[20] Opposition media outlets extensively covered these rallies. Organizers, as well as participants, were detained mostly during unauthorized gatherings, such as Strategy-31 rallies.[21]

Events peaked in February and began to decline thereafter. One of the most significant anti-government protests occurred on February 4 at Bolotnaya Square, where people rallied against electoral manipulation. This event had participants from over 100 cities. At the same time, a pro-Putin rally took place in another location at Poklonnaya Gora. This rally, believed to be backed by the regime, also drew tens of thousands of attendees. However, there were allegations that some participants were coerced or paid to attend.

Leading up to the presidential election on March 4, pro-government rallies, which were suspected to be orchestrated by the regime – given numerous reports of pressure on public sector workers and students – also took place.[22]

---

[20] Stanislav Markelov was a Moscow Human Rights Centre lawyer, while Anastasia Baburova was an environmental activist. Both were murdered in Moscow in January 2009.

[21] Strategy-31 was a social movement advocating for the right to assemble peacefully as per Article 31 of the Constitution in a series of events held on the 31st of every thirty-one-day month (Gabowitsch, 2018).

[22] The topic of pro-government mobilization in Russia is not extensively covered in this Element. However, it represents a significant and understudied aspect of contentious politics. Due to the reported use of intimidation, coercion, and monetary incentives, coupled with the government's control over ensuring extensive media coverage of these events, it is classified as one of the attributes of authoritarian innovation.

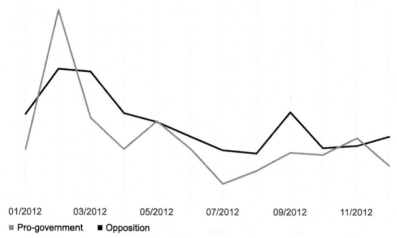

01/2012   03/2012   05/2012   07/2012   09/2012   11/2012
■ Pro-government   ■ Opposition

Figure 6 The trends of opposition and pro-government events in 2012.
Note: Pro-government events support Putin, United Russia, and state politics or oppose claims made against the state (e.g., rallies against electoral manipulation rallies).

While pro-government demonstrations are not new to Russian contentious action, their frequency significantly increased during this period, as illustrated in Figure 6. This suggests the regime's attempts to use these events to demonstrate its support during heightened contention.

In the wake of the presidential election in March 2012, the focus of the claims shifted toward Vladimir Putin and alleged electoral manipulation. Simultaneously, the regime altered its response to opposition movements. Detentions intensified, especially during larger unauthorized events. The Pushkinskaya Square event on March 5 was particularly notable due to the extensive detentions and confrontations between law enforcement and rally participants.

As police actions became more restrictive, contentious events diminished in April. Significant incidents, such as a Red Square rally and a demonstration against Arctic drilling, concluded with multiple detentions. There were also pro-government rallies against opposition rallies in Moscow, reportedly organized by families of OMON officers. Prominent opposition figures and organizers, including Ilya Yashin, Sergey Udaltsov, and Alexey Navalny, were frequently detained and fined. As detentions increased and event authorizations declined, political persecution continued, while events directly challenging the regime saw a drop in frequency. Pro-government events decreased rapidly after the presidential election, mirroring a similar decline in contentious events organized by the opposition.

May 2012 became the next milestone for the opposition. Contentious actions saw a heightened regime response, culminating in the Bolotnaya Square event on May 6, titled the "March of Millions." It took place a day before Putin's inauguration. Although initially authorized, the march was marred by barriers, clashes, and over 400 detentions when organizers refused to alter the route of their march following police intervention. This event signified a major change in the regime's response, especially compared to previous events from 2011–2012. Organizers and opposition activists were detained, including Alexey Navalny, Boris Nemtsov, and Sergey Udaltsov. Participants, who wore white ribbons, a symbol of the opposition movement, faced intensified police actions and sustained injuries. The regime also reported injuries among the law enforcement officers. Later, the Moscow mayor publicly rewarded the injured officers for their service by gifting them apartments.

In the days after the dispersal of the event, small-scale rallies, termed "festive walks," took place, resulting in more detentions and action from law enforcement officers. An indefinite sit-in, Occupy Abai, began on May 10 at Chisty Prudy Boulevard and extended to Saint Petersburg. This sit-in and subsequent rallies in Arbat, Kudrinskaya, and Barrikadnaya faced dispersals and detentions throughout May. At the same time, event organizers were repeatedly denied authorization to hold some of their proposed events, resulting in a rapid decline in their number in the forthcoming months.

Simultaneously, with the rise in repression, political persecution, and the number of detainees, the regime began implementing repressive legislation. It aimed to constrain citizens' participation in contentious events and limit general criticism of the government. These laws became the basis for detentions and investigations in the forthcoming years, targeting the limitation of expression and involvement in contentious events against the regime or specific social groups. Instead of outright banning certain activities, the federal government incrementally introduced restrictions that heightened the cost of participation and deterred certain forms of claim-making, with punishments becoming progressively more severe.

Several laws directly related to contentious events were passed, amending their procedural provisions. These amendments introduced new event authorization applications, accountability for multiple law violations, increased fines, and new items such as "a simultaneous presence of multiple individuals at a specific location." Another significant change was the introduction of the term "foreign agent," which would later become one of the main tools of repression and undergo numerous amendments and extensions over the following decade, primarily targeting the opposition.[23] The regime also introduced website blocklists and the term "intentional distribution of false information."[24]

Contention diminished over the following months with some claims against police violence. A March of Millions on June 12 transpired without incident, despite police raids on opposition leaders' homes the day before. Another March of Millions was also held in September, attracting thousands of participants. In October, elections to the opposition's coordination council took place. A support rally with around 1,000 participants was led by Sergey Udaltsov, who was detained later that month. He was interrogated regarding his alleged intentions to organize mass riots in collaboration with Leonid Razvozhaev and Konstantin Lebedev.

Over this post-Bolotnaya period, the authorities increasingly denied event authorization to arrange events in historically contentious areas, especially in Moscow. The difficulty of securing event permits became the primary concern for the opposition, with leaders opting for compliance to avoid detainments and preferring not to hold rallies and demonstrations without authorization. Continuing with the repressive legislation, the regime introduced revisions to the terms "state treason," "state secret," and "espionage." These changes broadened and generalized the definition of "state security" and its related terms in the Federal Law N190-FZ.

The year's final significant rally took place on December 15 in Lubyanka Square, drawing thousands of participants. This event led to the detentions of key opposition figures. Heightened security measures were noticeable in Moscow leading up to the event, indicating readiness to interfere.

4.2.2 2013: New Repressive Legislation and More Persecution

In January 2013, the frequency of contentious events and the number of detentions continued to decrease, as shown in Figure 7. One of the most notable events was a rally against the Dima Yakovlev Law, which prohibited US citizens from adopting Russian children.[25] Other events during this

---

[23] Foreign agents are organizations that either receive overseas funding or engage in activities considered political with overseas entities such as governments.

[24] Federal Laws N65-FZ, N121-FZ, N139-FZ, N141-FZ.

[25] The Dima Yakovlev law (N272-FZ) sanctioned US citizens whom the Russian regime accused of violating the human rights of Russian citizens abroad. Additionally, the law prohibited US citizens from adopting Russian children. This legislation was a response to the Magnitsky Act passed by the US Congress (Rouvinsky, 2021).

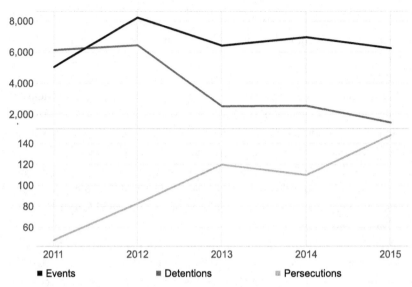

Figure 7 The number of new instances of reactive repression and political persecution in 2011–2015 compared to the general trend of contentious events.

period included commemorative rallies, LGBTQ+ support against upcoming restrictive laws, and worker movements.[26] The Strategy-31 event resulted in approximately thirty detentions, one of which was of their leader, Eduard Limonov.

The opposition criticized the authorities for increasingly denying permission for mass events. Meanwhile, Moscow designated specific areas for gatherings, prohibiting mass events outside these zones. OMON maintained a strong presence at subsequent Strategy-31 events and other rallies. The state authorized events by LDPR, CPRF, and environmental groups while also organizing rallies in support of the army, Vladimir Putin, and Dmitry Medvedev.

The first four months of 2013 saw multiple environmental rallies and smaller protests led by the opposition in support of political prisoners. Detentions occurred at Red Square for individuals carrying banners reading, "Down with Tsar Putin." Large rallies in May and June supported the Bolotnaya prisoners, drawing 30,000 participants on May 6 and June 12.

Law enforcement used force against contentious events opposing Putin's Plan Mosque and unauthorized rallies at Triumph Square. Moscow's Gay

---

[26] Law N135-FZ aims to protect children from information deemed harmful by classifying it as challenging "traditional family values." This categorization includes discussions related to nontraditional relationships, which affects the LGBTQ+ communities.

Pride was banned, and the regime declined permissions for other LGBTQ+ events. This prohibition preceded the introduction of new laws, N135-FZ and N136-FZ, banning "the propaganda of non-traditional sexual relationships." Additional provisions were added against "insulting believers' feelings" and "violations aimed at disrupting religious ceremonies." The opposition faced restrictions on rallies and refusals of event authorization. Detentions continued throughout the year during various unauthorized events.[27]

In December, the court was granted the authority to block websites deemed extremist based on a new definition, which includes calls for mass riots and a new concept of "extremist claims." Another law redefined the notion of "calls for violating territorial integrity." It limited citizens' freedom to express their opinions on specific political issues, including the events in Ukraine a few months later.[28]

4.2.3 2014: The Crimea Invasion

Throughout 2014, the dynamics of contentious events shifted. The period surrounding Russia's invasion of Crimea was characterized by numerous pro-government rallies that frequently overshadowed events organized by the opposition. The slight increase in large-scale events led to a marginal rise in detentions and reactive repression. However, even though there were more detainees in 2014 than in 2013, most contentious events unfolded peacefully.

On February 21, some opposition activists attempted to hold a rally in support of the Bolotnaya Case prisoners. However, the police restricted access to Manezhnaya Square, where the event was planned, preventing participants from taking any action. During the final court hearings related to the case, some activists gathered around the Zamoskvoretsky court, resulting in random detentions. After the 2012 Bolotnaya participants' conviction and the court's concluding statement, additional detentions took place on Tverskaya Street against people gathered to rally against the court's decision.

After the invasion of Crimea in March, localized anti-invasion demonstrations emerged throughout Russia, primarily in Moscow and Saint Petersburg. Significant events also took place in other major cities, such as Yekaterinburg and Samara. On March 8, left-wing affiliates gathered at Mars Field in Saint

---

[27] One of the most notable clashes took place in Biryulyovo, Moscow, following the murder of a young ethnic Russian, allegedly by an Azerbaijani immigrant. A gathering against perceived rising migrant crime escalated into violent clashes with the police, alongside attacks on properties associated with migrants. The authorities responded by deploying OMON and detaining 400 participants. The total number of participants was estimated at 2,000–6,000.

[28] Laws N398-FZ and N433-FZ.

Petersburg for an authorized rally. March 15 saw the nationwide "March of Peace," which coincided with even larger pro-government events.

The regime responded to protesters by making over 1,500 detentions over two months, predominantly in Moscow and Saint Petersburg. The occurrence of contentious events dipped between April and July 2014, replaced by demonstrations supporting media freedom, opposing construction projects like the Moscow–Kazan railway, advocating for environmental concerns like deforestation, and commemorating events like the deportation of Crimean Tatars' seventieth anniversary.

Repression heightened following the Crimea invasion, and cases of intimidation for making inappropriate remarks surged. Most of the political persecution cases in 2014 related to Ukraine and expressions of public support for it (OVD-Info, 2014). For instance, a Moscow State Institute of International Relations (MGIMO) professor was dismissed for refusing to recognize Crimea as part of Russia.

The regime continued to introduce repressive legislation throughout the year. In May, it outlawed denying or distorting the USSR's role in World War II. It also mandated owners of websites receiving more than 3,000 visitors to register with the Federal Service for Supervision of Communications, Information Technology, and Mass Media (Roskomnadzor). Additionally, the regime amended its constitution to include Crimea within the country's territory. In June, the Ministry of Justice was empowered to designate entities as foreign agents based on its discretion if any evidence of external funding was discovered. Additionally, media organizations were prohibited from being entirely owned by foreign entities, and the permissible portion of foreign investment was reduced.[29]

Penalties, as well as the potential for subsequent detention for repeated violations of Article 20.2, were escalated, enabling the regime to levy higher fines and arrest or prosecute individuals for consistent participation in contentious events under Article 212.1 with penalties of up to five years in prison. Until 2014, participants in mass events could be arrested only if the protest occurred near a nuclear plant. However, with the new legislation's introduction (N258-FZ), law enforcement officers were permitted to detain participants for recurring violations, accompanied by the potential for criminal prosecution for subsequent infractions.

In December, unauthorized rallies supporting Alexey Navalny ahead of his court hearing faced detentions. The police utilized crowd separation techniques

---

[29] Laws N7-FKZ, N97-FZ, N128-FZ, N305-FZ.

and preemptively blocked the event's official Facebook page, which marked another new development in the regime's repertoire of repression.[30]

4.2.4 2015: Nemtsov's Assassination

In 2015, contentious events relating to the Yves Rocher case persisted with some major rallies on January 15. Authorized events took place in Moscow and Saint Petersburg, opposing the court's decision to imprison Oleg Navalny and subject Alexey Navalny to a suspended sentence. January also witnessed a significant pro-government event: a large rally in Grozny against Charlie Hebdo's Muhammad caricatures. It was endorsed by the republic's president, Ramzan Kadyrov, who gathered hundreds of thousands of participants.

Overall, there were fewer contentious events in 2015. Issues addressed included environmental concerns like preserving the Troitsky forest, pro-government anti-Maidan rallies, and housing concerns, notably rallies held by currency mortgage borrowers. As indicated in Figure 7, the number of detentions during mass events and the number of events remained lower during this period.

After the assassination of Boris Nemtsov on February 27, commemorative marches were held nationwide.[31] Large peaceful marches on May 1 featured participants carrying portraits of Nemtsov, but state-controlled media largely ignored these. Tributes, such as floral offerings at the site of Nemtsov's murder, continued in the following months.

The number of new cases of political persecution continued to rise. Various laws were applied for political reasons, and there was an uptick in cases tied to support for Ukraine. Judicial persecution was also initiated for violating "state territorial integrity" through online posts and images. One example is the Daria Polyudova case, where she, one of the organizers of the Kuban federalization rally, was prosecuted on three counts of public calls for extremism, including the use of the internet as a tool to make extremist calls. Other cases were based on public displays of disrespect toward specific groups (under Article 148), overt public disrespect, participation in terrorist or extremist groups, and involvement in mass riots (under Article 212).

---

[30] Alexey Navalny faced allegations of embezzlement related to his business dealings with Yves-Rocher, a French company. The trial and subsequent investigation were reportedly fraught with violations, and many have criticized the case as politically motivated. Ultimately, Navalny received a suspended sentence of 3.5 years, while his brother, Oleg Navalny, was imprisoned (The Guardian, 2014).

[31] Boris Nemtsov, one of the most notable opposition figures in contemporary Russian history, was fatally shot on the Bolshoy Moskvoretsky Bridge near the Kremlin. This bridge has since become a significant site of remembrance, hosting annual rallies in his honor.

In May 2015, the concept of "undesired organizations" was introduced, defining such entities as threatening the state's safety and constitutional order. By July 2015, provisions were established for search engines to exclude false, outdated, or misleading information upon requests from law enforcement agencies.[32]

A large opposition rally named "Power Turnover" occurred in the Maryino residential area on September 20. This marked the first large-scale event held in a residential area of the capital. The organizers selected this location as the Moscow officials were reportedly unwilling to negotiate or approve any other sites in the city.

4.2.5 Regional Contention In 2011–2015

As illustrated in Figure 8, most Russian regions exhibited similar contentious trends in six out of eight regional clusters. The number of contentious events remained consistent, with some noticeable spikes occurring during significant political events. This suggests that many of the major events were organized countrywide. A decline in contentious events was observed after 2012 in the first four clusters, which is attributed to the observation that major contentious events are often organized by the same organizations with a regional presence across the country and are usually centered around specific issues or events.

The regions with the most contention, with more than 1,000 reports on contentious events, are Moscow, Saint Petersburg, Moscow Oblast, Sverdlovsk Oblast, Novosibirsk Oblast, and Krasnodar Krai. These regions fall into Clusters 1, 3, and 4. They exhibit significant similarities in trends of contention, particularly during periods when major opposition and pro-government events are held. Being relatively populous areas, the regions serve as the epicenters where most contentious events occur.

Clusters 5, 6, 7, and 8 exhibit fewer similarities to the first four clusters. Notably, Cluster 8 has only a few reports on events. This cluster comprises the national republics of Chechnya, Ingushetia, and Tyva, all of which have a long history of human rights violations, safety concerns, and distinct societal structures with significant national, religious, and cultural aspects (Amnesty International, 2012; Khovalyg, 2023; Marty, 2009). It sets them apart from other regions in Russia.

Opposition organizations are mainly absent in these republics, while activists and human rights organizations have a minimal presence and often face violence, including murder, disappearance, and torture. Due to the weak presence

---

[32] Laws N129-FZ and N264-FZ.

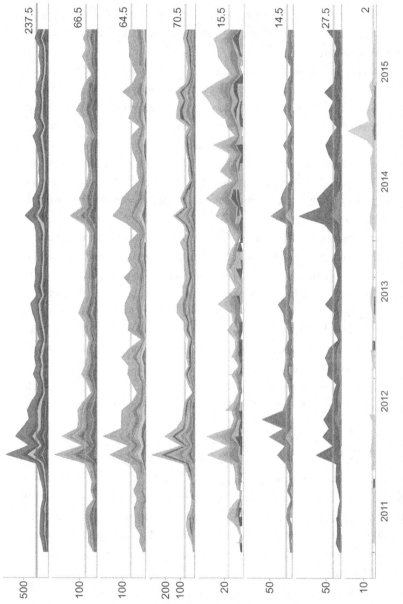

Figure 8 A comparison of contentious trends distributed among the eight clusters.

of human rights organizations and the ongoing threats from local authorities, as well as the social organization based on kinship systems, teips, and clans, instances of extrajudicial persecution often go unreported (Sokirianskaia, 2005, 2023). Such issues may be addressed through extrajudicial means and other extra-institutional bodies integrated within society. This makes the repression in these regions distinct from the rest of the country, reflecting the regions' contentious politics.

The data do not indicate significant contentious action in certain regions, including Mordovia, Amur Oblast, Sakhalin Oblast, Bryansk Oblast, and Smolensk Oblast. These regions, grouped in Cluster 6, exhibit irregular contentious patterns with missing reports for many dates. The data do not reveal a similar pattern of contention across these regions compared to the more populous clusters. For instance, despite its proximity to more contentious regions, Mordovia does not show comparable levels of contention, while Amur Oblast exhibits similar contentious patterns to Mordovia despite its geographic remoteness. This observation emphasizes the importance of organizational structures supporting contention, which tends to be absent in some regions.

Cluster 7 comprises Kalmykia, Nenets Autonomous Region, Magadan, and North Ossetia. While displaying slightly different trends, these regions share similarities with the least contentious regions from the other clusters. Most of these regions are geographically remote from Moscow and the other primary regions of the first four clusters. The impact of geographic remoteness on contentious action in Russia remains unclear. However, it should be noted that the least contentious regions during 2011–2015 also tend to be among the least populous. An additional observation is that these regions exhibit a higher number of pro-government events. In contrast, opposition events are seldom held.

Notable outliers exhibiting slightly different patterns of contentious events include Astrakhan Oblast. This region experienced a spike in such events in April when most other regions witnessed a decline. These events rallied around calls for free and fair elections and supporting Oleg Shein. Having lost the Astrakhan mayoral election, Shein announced a hunger strike, alleging that electoral manipulations denied him victory. Backed by the opposition and his party, Just Russia, several events were organized in his favor, subsequently dispersed by the police.

Thus, a majority of contentious events were concentrated within the first four clusters of regions. They displayed consistent patterns of contention, echoing significant political developments countrywide. The example of Astrakhan Oblast underlines that specific regional circumstances, such as mayoral elections, can be conducive to contention. Therefore, the influence of local politics and societal structures and their variations visibly impacted contentious action in Russian regions despite the overall uniform narrative.

4.2.6 Authoritarian Innovation and Contention in 2011–2015: Some Conclusions

The rise in contention during the State Duma and presidential elections prompted changes in the regime's response and its attempts to structure these reactions, as shown in Table 5. The regime's repressive strategies evolved through legislation that introduced new provisions and increased penalties for violating existing ones, focusing on deterrence and enhancing the capacity to repress future events. In terms of persecution, the regime targeted specific individuals and organizations that could potentially draw more participants and challenge it. Such individuals and organizations included political and religious movements and organizations classified as foreign agents. This shift signified a decreasing tolerance toward political claims against the regime.

The regime generally refrained from employing violence. The number of detentions fluctuated in correlation with the changes in contentious events, increasing and decreasing over time. Instead of violently dispersing rallies, the regime ensured its visible presence during all significant events by deploying substantial numbers of OMON and police troops, installing barriers, and restricting access to specific locations, a scenario primarily observed in Moscow.

Authorization for participation served as the regime's instrument to deter undesired events. While authorized contention witnessed minimal police intervention, most detentions occurred during unauthorized rallies, thereby increasing participation costs and discouraging the opposition from organizing them. Although some events proceeded without authorization, others were canceled due to the failure to secure an agreement with the officials, coupled with a desire to avoid endangering participants, consequently reducing contentious action. The authorities categorized detentions during unauthorized rallies as lawful, justifying the heavy presence of law enforcement officers, repressive actions, and portraying detainees as violators of legislation related to participation in mass gatherings.

Used in conjunction with the state-controlled media, the pro-government rallies demonstrated support for the regime during two of the significant political events of the period: the presidential election and the annexation of Crimea. By drawing more attention from the general public and its supporters, the regime ensured that these demonstrations were visible and their scope was emphasized. Meanwhile, using media blackouts and not reporting on events arranged by the opposition favored the pro-government events.

Table 5 Repressive strategies employed by the regime in 2012–2015

Repression	Strategy	Short description
Reactive	Detentions	Detentions prior to or during contention
	Dispersal techniques	Obstacles and tactics to encircle, divide, and disperse
	Violence	Physical damage inflicted on protesters
Proactive	Denial of event authorization	Discretionary rejection of event application
	Repressive legislation	New legislation imposing more restrictions on participation
	Political persecution	Politically motivated judicial persecution
	Police raids	Police raids and searches targeted at individuals or organizations to intimidate or persecute
	Heightened security measures	Increased police presence and blocking public access to specific locations
	Threats and intimidation	Threats and intimidation to deter participation
	Progovernment events	Events arranged by the government using coercion or monetary incentives for participants to support state politics
	Media blackouts	Intentionally underreporting contention
	Website blocklists	Limiting access to websites and social media pages

Another innovative attribute is the legislation introduced in response to specific events. For instance, laws concerning the violation of territorial integrity and undermining the role of the USSR in World War II were enacted during the annexation of Crimea, effectively preventing any criticism against this particular instance of authoritarian politics. These laws introduced severe punishments and were later used to prosecute activists. As Table 6 suggests, in most cases, the regime continued to employ extremist and terrorist legislation to persecute. The law against the propagation of nontraditional relationships significantly restricted the range of events the LGBTQ+ community could organize, while other laws limited what could be expressed and who could be criticized during contentious events. The regime also took initial steps toward controlling the nature of information being expressed online, outlining specific topics that could potentially cause repercussions.

Table 6 Political persecutions against individuals during 2011–2015 by Article from the Criminal Code

Article	Description	Count
282.2 Part 2	Participation in the activity of an extremist organization	94
282.2 Part 1	Organization of the activity of an extremist organization	69
205.5	Organization of or participation in a terrorist organization	56
30 Part 1	Preparations to commit a crime	54
213 Part 2	Hooliganism committed by a group	53
282 Part 1	Actions to incite hatred or enmity	49
278	Forceful seizure or retention of power	44
212 Part 2	Participation in mass riots	37
282	Incitement of hatred or enmity	29
318 Part 1	Use of violence against a public official or threats	29
205	Terrorism	23
30	Preparations to commit a crime	20
205.5 Part 1	Organizing activities of a terrorist organization	17
205.5 Part 2	Participation in activities of a terrorist organization	17
222 Part 3	Illegal acquisition, transfer, sale, storage, transport, or bearing of firearms and parts, ammunition, explosive substances, or explosive devices by an organized group	17

Source: Federal Protective Service of the Russian Federation (2023); OVD-Info (2023a)

The regime's innovative responses were often triggered by specific events occurring immediately after particular instances of contentious action. New amendments to the legislation, an increase in fines, and the expansion of grounds for arrests, as well as heightened punishments for individuals detained repeatedly, were introduced following major contentious events. The Bolotnaya case marked the first mass persecution of participants, demonstrating the regime's willingness to employ more repressive strategies and increase the participation costs for activists at its discretion whenever regime-imposed orders are disregarded. By placing restrictions on the most visible activists, introducing and showcasing the enforcement of new legislation, and preliminary detentions of prominent activists and their subsequent political persecution, the regime aimed to prevent and reduce their ability to organize further events.

Detentions, increased requirements for event authorizations, political persecutions of Bolotnaya participants, and new legislation significantly impacted the frequency and continuity of events held by the opposition. The continuous streak of rallies that commenced toward the end of 2011 and extended until April–May 2012 transitioned into less continuous and less frequent sudden spikes in contention during 2013–2015. No reports indicated any backlash and events dispersed by law enforcement officers did not resume later. The increased detentions were not met with violence, as no reports were suggesting the use of violence against law enforcement officers in general.

The repertoire of contention included rallies, marches, demonstrations, individual pickets, sit-ins, and strikes. Due to the regulatory nature of participation, events were typically held within specific time frames and at particular locations agreed upon with the officials, rarely deviating from the repertoire. The most significant events were organized by the noninstitutional opposition and the most prominent actors, who lawfully submitted authorization applications beforehand. It remains unclear whether a refusal to authorize an event would diminish the number of participants in 2011–2015. However, the decision to hold or cancel the event rested with the organizers, with participants generally adhering to the organizers' decisions and refraining from showing up if the event was canceled.

4.3 2016–2019: Heightened Repression

After a slew of new legislation, the regime reduced its legislative efforts and focused on the introduction of new repressive tools and ensuring control over the areas that were not under its control. In addition to already existing repressive strategies, the regime continued its innovation in the areas of political persecution and infringing on organizations and organizers taking part in contentious events. After a reduction in the number of events after 2012, the regime had to deal with several periods of heightened contention (Figure 9).

4.3.1 2016: Rosgvardia and the Yarovaya Law

In January 2016, several hundred participants attended an authorized event against repression in support of Ildar Dadin. He had been detained and convicted under Article 212.2 for repeatedly participating in unauthorized events, even though he was engaged in solo picketing at the time of his detention. He

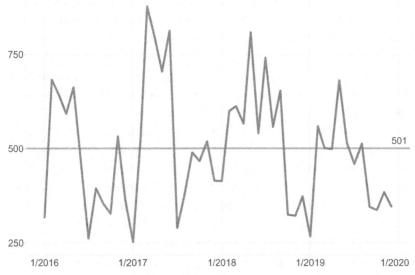

Figure 9 The state-wide number of reports on contentious events in 2016–2019.

was sentenced to three years in prison and became one of the most famous individuals persecuted for this reason.[33]

Overall, contentious actions of that period showed a heightened focus on specific issues rather than the broader political situation. Minor rallies against the bankruptcy of Transaero, issues faced by currency mortgage holders, paid parking, church construction, and other developmental projects around the country took place, similar to the repertoires of the previous years. There were gatherings in support of Crimea and environmental concerns, such as a rally in Dubki Park in Moscow or the "We Are Together" pro-government concert. Demonstrations against paid parking resulted in clashes and arrests. Contentious events erupted across Russia in response to the introduction of the Platon system. This system imposed additional taxes on trucks weighing more than twelve tonnes, leading to strikes by business owners and drivers. These confrontations eventually led to multiple detentions. During a rally marking the fourth anniversary of the Bolotnaya events, the participants were detained for holding signs that read, "Fabrication of the Bolotnaya case is a state crime" and "Free the heroes of May 6th."

---

[33] Ildar Dadin was the first individual to be sentenced to prison for repeatedly violating laws governing participation. Reports suggest correctional officers tortured and beat him on orders from the prison management (BBC News, 2016).

A significant development in the contentious politics of the regime in that period was the restructuring of the Ministry of Internal Affairs internal army, leading to the introduction of the National Guard (Rosgvardia). This new entity incorporated OMON and several other existing structures within the Ministry's internal army. Rosgvardia became an autonomous organization reporting directly to the president. It played a role during rallies, particularly in crowd dispersal, detentions, and the use of force (Galeotti, 2021).

The Yarovaya Laws became another milestone in the evolution of authoritarian repression.[34] Initially introduced as anti-terrorist laws, these regulations increased law enforcement officers' authority to access users' personal data. They also mandated internet providers to store traffic to identify extremist and terrorist organizations and communications to prevent potential terrorist acts. The laws decreased the age of criminal responsibility for crimes classified as terrorist acts and lowered the age of criminal responsibility regarding participation in mass riots. Messages on social networks that condoned terrorism were categorized as media publications and punished accordingly. Furthermore, religious organizations were stripped of their right to conduct missionary work unless they were officially registered and authorized to perform such activities.

The Society of Internet Defenders tried to organize a contentious event against the Yarovaya laws but was ultimately denied permission despite an initial authorization. Various related events occurred throughout Russia, with attendance ranging from tens to hundreds of participants.

4.3.2 2017: He Is Not Dimon to You

In 2017, there was a surge in large-scale contentious events, with reactive repression and detentions increasing even faster, as depicted in Figure 10. The overall number of contentious events remained limited while the opposition focused on organizing large-scale events. While some sought government authorization, there were instances, especially following criticism, where they attempted to hold these events without official approval. These unauthorized rallies led to heightened detentions and intensified confrontations with the regime.

In January and February 2017, issue-specific protests arose surrounding developmental and environmental concerns. Minor instances of contention occasionally led to detentions, such as during the January 14 rally in support of political prisoners. Several protests in Saint Petersburg, with 1,000–2,000

---

[34] Laws N374-FZ and N375-FZ.

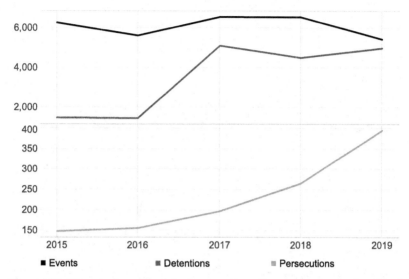

Figure 10 The number of new instances of reactive repression and political persecution in 2016–2019.

participants each, emerged against the transfer of Isaac's Cathedral to the ownership of the Russian Orthodox Church. Other parts of the country hosted commemorative events, as well as protests against infrastructure development and the decriminalization of domestic violence. In March 2017, major pro-government rallies took place nationwide, celebrating the annexation of Crimea, attracting tens of thousands of participants in total.

By 2017, many pro-government events had evolved into a more regular repertoire. Notably, from 2011 to 2015, such events typically coincided with periods of heightened contention. However, instead of being a response to heightened contention periods, pro-government rallies became regularly scheduled events annually commemorating specific dates, as shown in Figure 11.

On March 26, riot police were deployed at unauthorized rallies in Moscow and several other cities. Despite tens of thousands of participants nationwide, the lack of event authorization in most cities led to nearly 2,000 detentions. These rallies were organized in response to a video released by Alexey Navalny's Anticorruption Foundation, a national opposition organization dedicated to combating corruption in Russia. The video "He Is Not Dimon to You" exposed alleged wealth and corrupt ties among top state officials, including ex-president and the then prime minister Dmitry Medvedev. The creators of the video anticipated a reaction from the regime, but when none came, they organized the events. Concurrently, several employees from the Anticorruption Foundation were arrested.

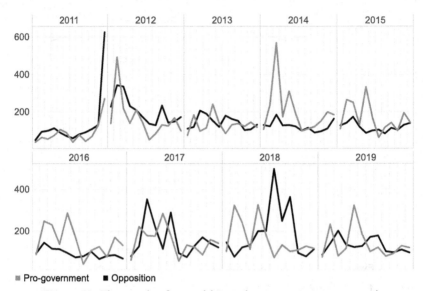

Figure 11 The trends of opposition and pro-government events in
2011–2019.

Smaller-scale anticorruption rallies were held after these events early in
April across the country by various organizations, including Yabloko, CPRF,
Russian National Front, and Citizen's Initiative. Some participants reported
state-initiated internet access blocks. Open Russia organized unsanctioned contention in several cities, some of which ended with dispersals and additional
detentions. In June, anticorruption rallies continued with increased participation and a rise in detentions, especially during some unauthorized events
in many of Russia's largest cities, drawing tens of thousands of participants.
Authorities used gas and force against participants at the Tverskaya Street
rally. Before the event, Alexey Navalny, the organizer, was detained and jailed
for thirty days for not adhering to the approved mass gatherings process; he
attempted to shift the venue from Sakharov Prospect to Tverskaya Street earlier
during another rally.

Overall, 1,800 people were detained nationwide. There was a significant rise
in detentions in Saint Petersburg, with around 700 arrests during a smaller,
unauthorized rally. Additionally, in June 2017, any gatherings organized by
political parties to engage with their electorate were classified as rallies and
pickets. These required prior approval to avoid being labeled as unsanctioned
mass events.

Following thousands of detentions, a rise in persecution, and increasingly
violent reactions from the regime, opposition rallies subsided. July and August
saw a sharp drop in the number of contentious events. There were smaller-scale

protests in support of Alexey Navalny across Russia, with gatherings in cities like Novosibirsk, Omsk, Kazan, and Yekaterinburg, among others.

In October 2017, more anticorruption action was scheduled in various cities across Russia. These events witnessed around 320 detentions during unauthorized and authorized rallies, with the total number of participants ranging from 10,000 to 20,000. Even though the event had not been officially authorized in Saint Petersburg, the police initially did not intervene. However, they later began dispersing the crowd, detaining approximately seventy participants. Several smaller events followed these incidents, eventually decreasing over the next weeks.

In November, several reports related to an alleged organization of mass nationalist events supporting Vyacheslav Maltsev, a rightist politician. Becoming a famous opposition activist, he advocated for a revolution in Russia. After multiple detentions and persecution as an extremist, he fled the country and announced a revolution on November 5, followed by Putin's impeachment. His supporters were detained and prosecuted as members of extremist organizations all over the country prior to, during, and after rallies that took place on November 5, with a reported number of 448 detainees around the country.

A distinctive feature of 2017 was the rise in cases related to Article 318, violence against a law enforcement officer. Most of these cases emerged following the anticorruption events in March. For example, seventeen-year-old Mikhail Galyashkin was accused of using pepper spray against an OMON officer. Yuri Kuliy was arrested and later found guilty, receiving an eight-month prison sentence for allegedly causing significant pain and physical harm by grabbing a police officer's arm.

4.3.3 2018: He Is Not a Tsar to Us and the Pension Reform

In 2018, the frequency and scale of contentious events marked it as one of the most eventful years, with Alexey Navalny and his Anticorruption Foundation leading the charge. In late January 2018, the Anticorruption Foundation organized demonstrations in some of the largest cities. These events followed the Central Electoral Commission's decision not to register Navalny for the upcoming presidential election, leading to a series of rallies dubbed the "Strikes of the Electorate." While many were authorized, contentious action in Moscow and Saint Petersburg was not due to disagreements over the location, which led to detentions. Before the rallies, several of Navalny's offices faced police raids.

In March, the regime organized a rally in support of Putin, attracting tens of thousands of attendees. Reports indicated that students, state workers, and pensioners were pressured or incentivized to attend. After the presidential election, minor political rallies were held around the country, claiming the results were falsified.

At the end of March, Kemerovo witnessed rallies following a fire at a local shopping mall. Claim-makers demanded a thorough investigation and accountability. Law enforcement officers were present but did not intervene. In solidarity, several rallies were organized nationwide, including in Moscow. A peaceful gathering with candles and flowers commemorated the fire's victims, explicitly stating there would be no political statements in the process.

On April 30, in response to the government's announcement to block Telegram, thousands took to the streets in Moscow, Saint Petersburg, and several other major cities, with the majority gathering in Moscow. The demonstrations, heavily promoted on Telegram and other social networks, were organized by the Libertarian Party and the Society for Internet Protection. The main rally was sanctioned by the officials and proceeded without detentions.

Contentious action continued in May with a series of large-scale contentious events named "He is not a Tsar to you" and organized by Alexey Navalny and his Anticorruption Foundation. In some regions, the organizers failed to obtain authorization from the officials but held gatherings nevertheless. Around 1,600 detentions occurred nationwide, with half coming from Moscow alone. Twenty-three journalists were arrested in the process.

The protests drew tens of thousands of participants. Some participants faced prosecution for violence against law enforcement officers. Both media and participants noted the presence of individuals dressed in Cossack attire at some events, who reportedly attacked and dispersed protesters.[35] Violence and multiple attacks on demonstrators were reported in Moscow and Saint Petersburg. Additionally, there was an increase in pro-government commemorative rallies in the Moscow Oblast related to Victory Day on May 9, indicating the regime's effort to draw more attention to the celebrations.

The next surge of contention happened against the pension reform throughout the country in July. The reform sought to raise the retirement age. These events were organized by various organizations and figures, including the CPRF, Just Russia, LDPR, Confederation of Independent Labor Unions of Russia, Anticorruption Foundation, Yabloko, and various leftist movements. A notable feature of the rallies was their widespread occurrence across Russia, with many occurring in regional areas. The announcement of the forthcoming

---

[35] Cossacks are ultrapatriotic groups with close ties to the regime, claiming descent from Tsarist horsemen. They have been known to intimidate and disperse protesters since 2012, especially in May 2018, although the authorities have purportedly denied any association with them.

pension reform coincided with the 2018 World Football Cup, which imposed restrictions on where contentious events could be held.

Among the largest rallies against this reform were those organized by the CPRF across the country; the most significant gathering attracted around 10,000 participants in Moscow, concluding without any detentions. However, a few arrests occurred during a rally organized by the Libertarian Party. Smaller events occurred from 2018 to 2019, with a noticeable decrease in participation numbers. The regime proceeded to approve the reform in October. Scattered detentions were documented in cities like Krasnodar, Moscow, and Saint Petersburg during nationwide rallies.

October to December saw events supporting political prisoners, particularly those involved in the "Network" and "New Greatness" cases. Both cases emerged as instances of political persecution against groups that made claims against the state. "Network" represented anti-fascist and anarchist factions from Penza. Its members were convicted based on alleged plans to execute acts of terrorism against the state. Meanwhile, participants of the "New Greatness" organization were labeled as extremists and were accused of plotting to overthrow the government. Both trials were marred with procedural violations and claims that existing evidence was fabricated. Some detainees alleged torture, but the regime rejected such accusations (OVD-Info, 2018, 2019).

4.3.4 2019: The Moscow Duma Election

In February, several rallies were held supporting political prisoners, commemorating Nemtsov, and democracy. Some events revolved around healthcare, housing, and environmental issues, including action against waste management policies, landfill sites, and construction on Lake Baikal, fueled by the 2019 garbage reform. The disputes related to the garbage reform persisted, especially in Archangelsk and the Moscow Oblast. Contention also arose from the ongoing closure of hospitals due to healthcare optimization reforms. Several people were detained on May 1 during labor demonstrations in Saint Petersburg and other cities. The regime labeled these events as "unauthorized activities within authorized ones," leading to over 100 detentions. This included activists from organizations like "Indefinite Protest," "Vesna," and "Open Russia" making political claims.

In the lead-up to the Moscow Duma elections and registration process, contention increased after opposition candidates faced difficulties when trying to register to participate in the election. Despite the officials' refusal to authorize, a rally was held on July 27. The organizers and opposition leaders, including Alexey Navalny, Ivan Zhdanov, and Ilya Yashin, were detained in advance and/or on the day of the event. In anticipation, the regime mobilized thousands of law enforcement personnel, including riot police. They restricted access to Tverskaya Street and managed crowds by separating groups of participants. It is estimated that at least 10,000 people participated. Throughout the day, 1,388 individuals were detained, with law enforcement using batons and force in some instances, which resulted in injuries. The authorities categorized the rally as a mass riot and subsequently prosecuted several attendees from among the detainees. In total, twenty-three individuals were charged with participating in mass riots and using violence against law enforcement officers. Despite the number of detentions and the officials' refusal to issue authorization, another unauthorized rally occurred on August 3. It saw over 1,000 detentions while participants intended to spread out across multiple locations to complicate detention efforts by law enforcement. Several reports emerged detailing injuries caused by law enforcement actions, with one injury reported from the police side.

On August 10, another major rally took place on Sakharova Avenue. It was an authorized event with an estimated 20,000–50,000 participants. However, after the rally concluded, 200 individuals were detained. This group had chosen to proceed toward the presidential administration building, which was not on the list of authorized locations on the application form. Some participants reported difficulties accessing the internet. Meanwhile, an unauthorized rally in Saint Petersburg attracted 200 attendees, of which 79 were detained.

On August 31, unauthorized gatherings occurred in Moscow and Saint Petersburg, yet no detentions were made. In September, another elections-related event was held in Moscow, which the officials authorized. This gathering saw around 20,000 participants, including many opposition leaders who could not attend some of the previous events.

4.3.5 Regional Contention in 2016–2019

As in 2011–2015, most clusters repeated the trends of contention, indicating the presence of countrywide rallies organized by the regime and major political parties, the Anticorruption Foundation, and other opposition organizations. However, compared to the previous period, 2016–2019 saw slightly more diversity and regional variation in contention. While the monthly median of reports on contention declined in some of the clusters, other regions showed slightly different patterns of contention and even increases in such instances, as shown in Figure 12.

The regions with the most contention included Moscow, Moscow Oblast, Saint Petersburg, Novosibirsk Oblast, Sverdlovsk Oblast, and Krasnodar Krai

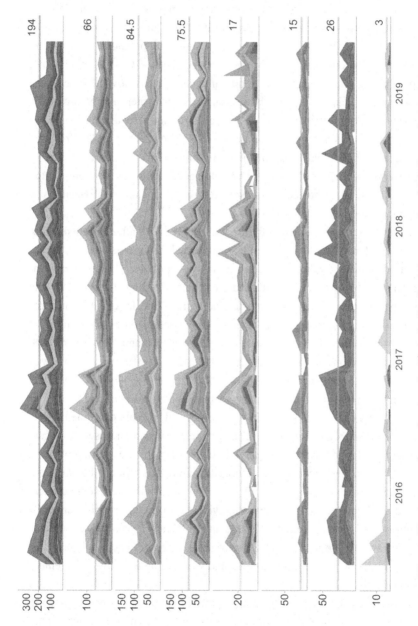

Figure 12 A comparison of contentious trends distributed among the eight clusters in 2016–2019.

from Clusters 1, 3, and 4. The differences among the clusters are notable during 2016 when the incidence of countrywide contention was relatively lower in general, but issue-specific contention persisted, for example, rallies related to labor and environmental issues in Samarskaya Oblast and notably in Tolyatti, as well as environmental and commemorative rallies in Moscow Oblast.

Clusters 5, 6, 7, and 8, mainly comprising less populous regions and republics, were dominated by pro-government actors. On the other hand, despite having a low number of reports in general, Khabarovsk Krai showed several events related to local issues, such as hot water supply problems, increasing costs of utilities, and threats to the region's biodiversity and living conditions. A similar trend can be observed in Astrakhan Oblast from the same cluster. Tula Oblast, one of the more contentious regions in Cluster 7, saw several commemorative rallies and state-sponsored demonstrations related to history. Chechnya hosted state-sponsored rallies in support of Muslims in Myanmar and on National Unity Day.

Contentious action erupted in Ingushetia in 2018–2019 after Chechen leader Ramzan Kadyrov and Ingush president Yunus-bek Evkurov signed an agreement to demarcate the borders between the two republics. These rallies gathered tens of thousands of people and were authorized by the officials. The claim-makers criticized the regime for the secrecy and lack of communication with the republic's populace when deciding to cede some of the republic's territory to Chechnya. After several rallies in October and November 2018, new demonstrations emerged on March 26, 2019. This resurgence followed the regional government's amendment to the legislation, which removed the requirement to hold a referendum when demarcating territories, and the failure to make any progress using appeals to the court and federal government.

A new phase began on March 27 after the participants refused to vacate the square following the authorized rally the day before. Rosgvardia officers, brought in from neighboring federal subjects, initiated the dispersal of the event and detained some participants. This action met with resistance; some officers refused to follow orders and detain individuals. In the aftermath, numerous organizers and participants were raided and politically persecuted in a series of cases named "The Ingush Case," resulting in prison sentences on charges of extremism, participation in mass riots, and violence against law enforcement officers (Novaya Gazeta, 2021).

In response, the government outlawed traditional organizations organizing the rallies, such as the Council of Teips. Hearings were conducted outside the republic in other Russian regions like Stavropolye and Kabardino-Balkaria to mitigate potential interference in the prosecution by local teips and connections. These events exemplify how instances of contention are suppressed with federal government involvement when regional authorities cannot do so themselves.

In 2016–2019, contentious action in Russia remained concentrated in specific regions. While local political developments and issues were conducive to contention in regions like Ingushetia and Moscow, the contentious trends in most regions mirrored the events observed in more populous clusters. This suggests a dependency on specific countrywide organizations when organizing contentious events. Regions traditionally experiencing more rallies shaped the countrywide dynamics, highlighting the centralized nature of such actions and the influential role of the federal center in conjunction with countrywide repression. In contrast, local organizational structures, if present, did not appear to contribute to contention significantly. Local bodies like the Council of Teips played their roles in regional rallies. However, members of such organizations face persecution while the regime demonstrates a willingness to intervene whenever local governments fail to control contentious action.

4.3.6 Authoritarian Innovation and Contention in 2016–2019: Some Conclusions

While the number of events did not change significantly compared to the 2011–2015 period, the regime resorted to repression more frequently during 2016–2019, targeting political organizations, individuals, and activists during unauthorized contention. By employing a wider range of legal instruments to persecute those who engaged in contentious action, the regime aimed to prevent their further involvement. This strategy narrowed the gap between the event incidence and the average number of detentions per event, as it was shown in Figure 10.

Organizers of contentious events encountered an increasing number of refusals when seeking authorization for particular events, while the regime increased the presence of law enforcement with full riot ammunition at all major contentious gatherings. Although the officials still permitted certain events, they became less willing to do so while introducing more stringent event authorization requirements. Faced with numerous refusals, the opposition opted to hold unauthorized events. This shift led to an increase in detentions and more frequent episodes of violence, actions which the authorities justified as lawful measures to prevent dissent. Detainees and political prisoners reported numerous instances of violence and torture during persecution, a particularly pronounced trend in 2018–2019.

Besides the increase in detentions and violence, the regime marked further steps toward tighter control over civil liberties by introducing the Yarovaya Law. Other notable developments included more frequent police raids and the utilization of extra-institutional actors to disperse participants. Within this period, the first cases occurred that classified participation in contentious events as a criminal offense. Much like before, the regime reacted with innovation to contention. It also resorted to persecution whenever significant rallies occurred. The regime took steps to heighten fines and modify legislation, attempting to deter both participants and organizers from contentious action. By targeting particular individuals and organizations, authorities sought to reduce the number of claim-makers and impede their capacity to hold larger events.

The regime employed newer techniques such as blocking internet access during major contentious events, executing preliminary detentions of activists, and conducting raids on their homes and offices. It also targeted organizations engaged in political activism. The regime shifted away from organizing pro-government rallies as a countermeasure to the opposition, instead focusing on deploying mechanisms that would undermine organizational structures and persecute more prominent opposition leaders. As depicted in Table 7, the regime escalated the degree of repressive tools previously used, introducing additional components to the existing strategies, such as using tear gas and force against nonviolent events and the criminal conviction of repeatedly detained activists.

The total number of persecutions markedly increased, with a two- or three-fold rise in the charges related to extremism and participation in terrorist organizations, as illustrated in Table 8. The regime sharpened its focus on employing extremist and terrorist legislation to politically persecute individuals. Additionally, there was a substantial increase in cases initiated based on violence against a public official.

The repertoires of contentious action remained consistent, with most larger events being organized nationwide, primarily by the Anticorruption Foundation and other organizations. Protesters did not engage in violent action, and organizers continually emphasized the importance of adhering to the democratic process, drawing a parallel to the repressive stance of the regime. Although the frequency of events declined, no significant change in their repertoires was observed. Attempts to organize more continuous events either lacked support from the participants or were dispersed by law enforcement officers. Organizers often chose specific dates for their actions and rarely acted without planning ahead. The officials allowed certain events but ensured they were of limited duration. Participants generally complied with legal requirements and procedures. They avoided engaging in specific acts that could incriminate them or draw undue attention from the regime. The decline in the number of events in 2019 was accompanied by an increase in detentions and repression, contrasting with the simultaneous decrease in both participation and detentions observed during the 2015–2016 period.

Table 7 Repressive strategies employed by the state in 2016–2019 redefined according to changes implemented by the state if compared to 2011–2015

Repression	Strategy	Definition
Reactive repression	Detentions	Detentions prior to or during contention followed by arrests and legal action
	Barriers, zoning, and dispersal techniques	Obstacles and tactics to encircle, divide, and disperse
	Violence	Physical damage, torture, the use of tear gas and force, including non-institutional actors for dispersal of nonviolent gatherings
	Blocked internet access	Blocked access to internet and cellular services during contention
Proactive repression	Event authorization	Discretionary rejection of applications, increasing requirements to gain authorization, including restrictions on location
	Repressive legislation	New legislation imposing more restrictions on participation
	Criminalization of participation	Repeated participation in contentious events classified as a criminal offense
	Political persecution	Politically motivated judicial persecution
	Police raids	Police raids and searches targeted at individuals or organizations for intimidation or further persecution
	Heightened security measures	Increased police presence and blocking public access to specific locations
	Threats and intimidation	Threats and intimidation to deter participation
	Pro-government events	Events arranged by the state using coercion or monetary incentives for participants
	Media blackouts	Intentionally underreporting contentious events
	Website blocklists	Limiting access to websites and social media pages
	Digital surveillance	Legal and technical mechanisms to store and access personal data by law enforcement officers

Table 8 Political persecutions against individuals during 2011–2015 by Article from the Criminal Code

Article	Description	Count
282.2 Part 2	Participation in the activity of an extremist organization	227
282.2 Part 1	Organization of the activity of an extremist organization	171
205.5 Part 2	Participation in activities of a terrorist organization	139
30 Part 1	Preparations to commit a crime	96
318 Part 1	Use of violence against a public official or threats	68
278	Forceful seizure or retention of power	52
205.5 Part 1	Organizing activities of a terrorist organization	49
282.3	Financing an extremist organization	47
282 Part 1	Actions to incite hatred or enmity	46
282.2	Organization of the activity of an extremist organization	37
212 Part 2	Participation in mass riots	31
205.1 Part 2	Inciting, recruitment, and other attempts to involve individuals in a terrorist organization using their position as an official	30
205	Terrorism	29
205.5	Organization of or participation in a terrorist organization	27
205.4 Part 2	Participation in a terrorist organization	25

Source: Federal Protective Service of the Russian Federation (2023); OVD-Info (2023a)

4.4 2020–2023: Full-Scale Repression

In 2020–2023, the regime escalated its repression and political persecution (Figure 13). Building on the repressive measures that had been put in place over the previous years, the regime adopted even more restrictive legislation and intensified its use of violence against the opposition. Prominent organizations and leaders were directly targeted, with many either incarcerated or compelled to leave Russia. Consequently, there was a notable decline in contention. By the year 2023, overt contentious activity and active political participation were effectively suppressed.

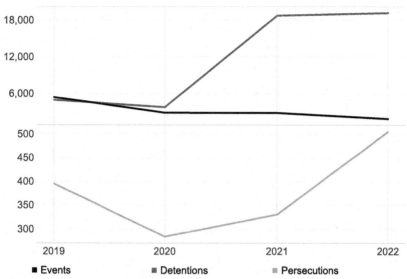

Figure 13 The number of new instances of reactive repression and political persecution in 2020–2022.

Note: The year 2023 is not shown due to only partially available data until March 2023.

4.4.1 2020: COVID Restrictions on Participation

As illustrated in Figure 14, contention declined in 2020 due to the introduction of anti-COVID measures and restrictions on public gatherings. Individual pickets emerged as the dominant form of claim-making because they allowed participants to comply with the social distancing requirements. Generally, the regime did not authorize rallies and gatherings and imposed strict repression whenever an unauthorized event took place. Participants in single-person pickets were often detained irrespective of their actions.

In 2020, a significant decrease in new political persecution cases occurred alongside a general decline in contentious actions and detentions. Article 212.2 on violating the procedure for organizing or holding public gatherings was applied against participants of contentious events in North Ossetia, who took it to the streets despite COVID restrictions and were violently suppressed. Several instances of 282.2 were initiated in February in the Jewish Autonomous Oblast, Khakassia, Primosky Krai, and Moscow.

In March, multiple pickets around the country opposed the announced reset of Putin's presidential term and constitutional amendments. The president redefined his presidential term, enabling him to participate in the upcoming presidential election. Additionally, the president retained the right to hold a

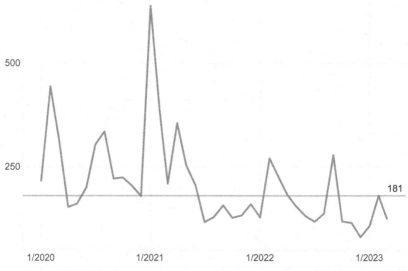

500

250

181

1/2020   1/2021   1/2022   1/2023

Figure 14 The state-wide number of reports on contentious events in
2020–2023.

lifelong senator position in the parliament, ensuring legal immunity and protection from prosecution. He also gained the authority to dismiss both prime
and federal ministers.[36] Although some groups applied for rally permits to
oppose the amendments, the officials declined these requests, citing the onset of
the COVID pandemic. Despite these restrictions, smaller events persisted with
numerous detentions. In addition to the regular enforcement of Article 20.2,
Articles 20.6.1 and 6.3 were invoked against detainees for violating quarantine
measures.

The regime also introduced a new N100-FZ law that penalizes the public
dissemination of intentionally false information about circumstances that pose
a threat to citizens' lives and safety, specifically in the context of the emergence
of COVID-19. The law also enhances the consequences for actions that create
a "threat of mass illness," such as organizing a rally during an epidemic.

One of the most notable events occurred in Vladikavkaz, attracting several
thousand participants. Arranged in April, this event led to numerous detentions and some injuries to Rosgvardia officers. Around 200 arrests were made
both before and after the event, resulting in multiple cases filed under Article
318 for violence against law enforcement officers. Another series of prolonged
environmental rallies aimed at protecting Shies unfolded in Archangelsk,
concluding in June when a decision was made to halt the construction.

---

[36] Law N1-FKZ.

On July 1, the day the constitutional amendments were signed, several hundred people gathered at Pushkinskaya without any subsequent detentions. Two weeks later, over 100 individuals were detained in Moscow for participating in an unauthorized protest regarding the same matter while also showing support for protesters in Khabarovsk and Belarus. From September to December, some detentions occurred at Moscow rallies, with attendance ranging from tens to hundreds of individuals. In 2020, about 800 protesters and individuals picketing alone were detained nationwide, leading to over 2,400 convictions under Article 20.2.

In July, contentious action began in Khabarovsk to support the detained governor Sergey Furgal and persisted throughout the year. Tens of thousands took to the streets in response. Despite many of these rallies and marches being unauthorized, law enforcement officers largely refrained from intervening during their peak. However, detentions started increasing in August as the number of participants declined and the issues highlighted by the claim-makers diversified, influenced by the political unrest in Belarus and the poisoning of Alexey Navalny.[37] Regions neighboring Khabarovsk expressed support for the protestors and advocated on behalf of the participants. On October 10, Rosgvardia intervened, using force to disperse the crowd and detaining approximately thirty individuals. Those not detained during the incident faced persecution in the days that followed.

New regulations related to the organization of rallies were introduced through N497-FZ. This law expands the definition of a "public event" to include "mass simultaneous presence and/or movement of citizens," necessitating approval from authorities. Furthermore, the term "public event" has been broadened to cover single pickets, previously the only form of contention that did not require approval. Another law, N541-FZ, imposes further restrictions on funding public events. It prohibits receiving funds for organizing public events from foreign governments, organizations, international entities, foreign nationals, "foreign agents," and anonymous donors if the event's attendance exceeds 500 people. The officials also reserve the right to reject a proposed location for an event and may suggest alternative venues. If the organizers deem these alternative locations unsatisfactory, their application to organize an event may be denied.

---

[37] In August, Navalny fell seriously ill from poisoning during a trip to Tomsk. He was first admitted to a hospital in Omsk before being transferred to Berlin. In September, tests conducted by international laboratories determined that Navalny was poisoned with a nerve agent from the Novichok group. The poisoning was later linked to Russia's Federal Security Service.

Further restrictions were introduced on foreign agents, including criminal charges for violations related to providing appropriate documentation. Their participation in the election process was limited; they were required to disclose their status before an election to be eligible to vote, and mandatory financial reporting requirements were imposed. The definition of foreign agents was expanded to encompass entities that gather data for a foreign source. Additionally, a new provision was introduced, mandating the referencing and description of the foreign agents' status when citing materials they produced.[38]

4.4.2 2021: Alexey Navalny's Imprisonment

Following the introduction of new repressive legislation and prohibitions in 2021, coupled with partially lifted restrictions on mass events, the year emerged as one of the most repressive of the previous decade. The largest contentious events occurred in Moscow on January 23 and again on January 31 and April 21.[39]

On January 23, more than 100,000 people took to the streets around the country in the majority of larger cities, with tens of thousands of participants in Moscow and Saint Petersburg and thousands of protesters in Perm, Yekaterinburg, Nizhny Novgorod, and Krasnodar, among others. Detentions began prior to the formal start of the event. It was not authorized in most regions, which resulted in multiple detentions of organizers, reports of problems with cellular networks, and access to the internet at the venues in multiple cities. The total number of detentions exceeded 4,000, with numerous injuries inflicted by law enforcement officers on participants and 70 people reporting injuries from twenty-three cities, particularly in Moscow and Saint Petersburg.[40] Several cases were later initiated for the use of alleged violence against law enforcement officers.[41] New legislation was utilized to prosecute participants of mass

---

[38] Laws N14-FZ, N481-FZ, N482-FZ, N525-FZ.

[39] These events were triggered by Navalny's return to Russia on January 17. He was immediately detained and subsequently imprisoned. The events were further fueled by the release of a video by the Anticorruption Foundation, implicating Putin and numerous top officials and businessmen in the largest corruption scheme in Russia's history.

[40] One of the most widely discussed incidents was an attack committed by a law enforcement officer in St. Petersburg who kicked Margarita Yudina in the stomach. She was hospitalized and complained to the Investigative Committee of Russia. She further faced threats and intimidation from the police and Child Safety Services, who threatened to look into her relationships with her children and how she treated them.

[41] Another notable case invoked an article on deliberate destruction of property against a Tik-Tok blogger Konstantin Kiyevsky, whose house was raided after he had snowballed a Federal Security Services vehicle during a rally. He was made to apologize in a video, was reportedly beaten by law enforcement officers, and received a sentence of two years and seven months in prison.

events, such as creating an epidemiological threat during a pandemic and obstructing traffic flow. More than fifty journalists were detained, and several were reportedly beaten.

Detentions continued during the subsequent event on January 31. Arrests and searches preceded the planned rallies. Journalists and activists were targeted ahead of the demonstrations. Sergey Smirnov, the chief editor of "Meduza," was detained due to alleged rally-related posts. Police issued warnings to journalists against participating in contentious events. Authorities employed strategies to block access to contention sites, leading to scattered demonstrations.

In Moscow and St. Petersburg, protesters evaded blockades through live coordination by Navalny's associate, Leonid Volkov. Some cities lacked backup plans, resulting in confusion and clashes with the police. Participants were beaten, dragged, and detained, with journalists also being targeted. The police employed batons, electroshock weapons, and other equipment, such as fire extinguishers. The number of detainees reached 5,754, with at least 63 of them reporting injuries. On February 2, more people were detained after the court sentenced Navalny to two years and eight months in prison; 370 detainees were reported near the courthouse, and 1,512 detentions were recorded in Moscow, Saint Petersburg, and other areas in total. In total, the events in support of Navalny resulted in over 11,400 detentions. There were reports that the police visited the homes of rally participants who were identified after the events using street cameras.

In February, smaller-scale events continued around the country, with a decrease in the number of participants. A large pro-government rally was held in March. Other notable issues included protests related to environmental issues, construction, and commemoration events. Commemoration rallies for Nemtsov were not authorized around the country, including Moscow, and some detentions occurred against individuals who attended these unauthorized events.

Contention on April 21 witnessed tens of thousands of people gathering around the country, with more than fifteen cities where the number of participants exceeded 1,000. Students were preliminarily notified about the possible consequences of participating in such gatherings, while preemptive detentions and police searches were conducted nationwide. The most violent and numerous detentions occurred in Saint Petersburg, with around 2,000 detainees all over the country. Notably, there was a reduction in repression in Moscow.

The forms of repression used by the regime included firing individuals (e.g., mass dismissal of Moscow metro workers), threats, closure of organizations, and designations of foreign agents or undesirable organizations. Concerns grew over Navalny's health in prison. The Prosecutor's Office sought to label Navalny's organizations extremist. The activities of his Anticorruption Foundation were suspended, leading to shutdowns of the regional headquarters. Increased scrutiny and arrests affected the Anticorruption Foundation's staff nationwide.

After the rallies, police utilized camera footage to identify participants and take legal action against them. Authorities in Moscow and Nizhny Novgorod employed facial recognition technology for identification. Prominent figures, including doctor Alexey Golovenko and writer Dmitry Bykov, were accused based solely on camera recognition results. Around thirty-five protesters from the April 21 rally were arrested using this method.

The police targeted journalists covering the rallies, utilizing strict regulations. New rules mandated the press to wear distinctive badges and vests with press markings. Despite these measures, some reporters were still confronted by police. Journalists like Anna Loyko and Alexey Korostelev were questioned or detained for alleged participation despite possessing press credentials. The regulations had been tightened earlier, requiring journalists to wear distinct identifiers provided by the officials.

Following the mass detentions, persecutions, and refusals to permit rallies, the number of contentious instances fell in the subsequent months. Some unauthorized protests, commemorative World War II activities, and environmental concerns persisted over May–June. In July, the Communist Party of the Russian Federation (CPRF) organized events opposing mandatory vaccination, addressing concerns about the epidemiological situation. Rallies were also conducted in support of political prisoners.

In July, the law N278-FZ prohibiting the comparison of the USSR and the Third Reich was enacted. This law forbids publicly equating the "objectives, decisions, and actions" of the USSR leadership with those of Nazi Germany and denying the "decisive role of the Soviet people in the defeat of Nazi Germany and the humanitarian mission of the USSR in liberating European countries." Another law, N424-FZ, broadened the circumstances under which police are permitted to break into a car, such as if there are "stolen items" inside, a suspect is locked inside, or passengers are "in danger." The authority to break into apartments has also been expanded.

In the lead-up to the State Duma elections in September, numerous events took place in August and September to protest the removal of certain candidates from the election or the refusal of their registration. Following the election, several social movement organizations and political parties attempted to organize contentious events to push back against the online voting system's introduction and challenge the election results. Security measures were intensified, and several pro-government events were held in response to support the regime.

4.4.3 January 2022–March 2023: The Invasion of Ukraine

Immediately following the full-scale invasion of Ukraine in 2022, several laws were introduced. Throughout the year, the government passed a total of 653 legislative acts, compared to 506 laws a year earlier. A distinctive characteristic of this period is the swift passage and subsequent enforcement of these laws to prosecute citizens. Concurrently, the regime continued its strategies used over the last decade, encompassing dispersion, prohibition, and persecution.

The year 2022 witnessed an unprecedented increase in detentions and heavy repression, accompanied by new laws and restrictions on public gatherings. Toward the end of February, following the invasion of Ukraine, unauthorized anti-war events and pickets emerged across the country, exhibiting a high level of participation. There were preliminary detentions targeting potential claim-makers and opposition leaders. The first war-related reports of contentious events surfaced before the invasion on February 19. On February 24, arrests occurred at pickets in major cities, including Moscow and Saint Petersburg.

The beginning of Russia's invasion of Ukraine on February 24 contributed to further restrictions and repression. The opposition, journalists, and activists voiced opposition to the war through open letters, protests, and social media. However, authorities countered efforts to criticize the invasion with censorship, repression, and arrests. Independent media outlets were blocked, and social platforms were restricted. Over 14,000 detentions were registered during rallies. By March 10, 712 participants faced administrative arrests, and 27 faced criminal charges. Most detentions occurred in the first month following the invasion, totaling 15,353 detainees, with more than 4,000 additional detentions in the subsequent year.

During anti-war protests, OVD-Info documented over 413 cases of police employing force, including beatings, choking, and inflicting injuries. Detainees endured various forms of violence, with incidents of fractures, dislocations, and head injuries reported. On several occasions, police denied medical assistance to the injured. Law enforcement officers arrested and detained individuals for expressing their views online, with over 2,000 cases wherein such posts were cited. With the onset of war, extrajudicial pressure associated with political beliefs intensified. Uninvestigated attacks and threats against claim-makers often remained unpunished, and other forms of pressure, such as job loss and social media bans, also went unaddressed. A substantial number of internet websites were blocked, while foreign and opposition media were compelled to either shut down or relocate overseas. Amid the war, authorities used facial recognition for preemptive arrests of activists.

In general, the anti-war protests were peaceful. People gathered in central city squares, some holding placards with calls for peace or expressions of support for Ukraine. Many attended without any promotional materials, simply showing up with small badges on their clothes or bags and still being detained. The events were not organized by a particular social movement organization, and people picketed at multiple locations simultaneously. In anticipation of protests occurring, law enforcement officers' presence often exceeded the actual number of claim-makers as a preliminary measure.

Claim-makers gathered for rallies in the following days, such as a demonstration at Gostinny Dvor in Saint Petersburg with several hundred participants and in Novosibirsk with around 400 participants simultaneously. Initially authorized, the officials withdrew the authorization in anticipation of the events to hold rallies commemorating Boris Nemtsov. On March 18, at Luzhniki stadium, the regime arranged an event with reportedly 200,000 attendees.

Legislation known as the "Law on Fakes" or "Law on War Censorship" in N31-FZ, N62-FZ, and N260-FZ amended the Criminal Code to incorporate penalties for discreditation and public actions directed against the Russian Army. A new addition to the Administrative Code of Russia was introduced (N32-FZ), imposing fines for violating these provisions. Dissemination of false information, actions discrediting the military, and calls for introducing restrictive measures (i.e., sanctions) against Russian citizens could be potentially classified as criminal offenses and lead to incarceration. These laws have been criticized as repressive due to their overgeneralization and the lack of clarity regarding what constitutes such violations, leading to their application in instances where they may not be applicable or where evidence is not definitive. As a result, these regulations were utilized to persecute citizens who publicly expressed their opinions.

From the mass rallies and demonstrations of the previous period, events transitioned primarily to picketing as the main form of contention. A subsequent surge in contentious activity was reported in September following the announcement of partial mobilization to enlist more soldiers for participation in the Ukraine war. Areas where contentious events might occur were preemptively blocked by the police, accompanied by a substantial presence of law enforcement officers. In the lead-up to the mobilization announcement, repetitive pro-government events were observed, culminating in a large rally on September 30, arranged to support the annexation of the Ukrainian territories. Following the announcement of partial mobilization, detentions surged across various locations throughout the country, totaling 1,369 detainees. On

September 24 alone, more than 833 detentions were made. Additionally, 176 organizations were designated as foreign agents.

A further reduction in contentious events was observed from October to December. Reports emerged indicating that police dispersed a contentious event opposing a construction project in Moscow, suggesting a shift toward a zero-tolerance approach toward any form of contention.

Following the invasion of Ukraine in 2022 and into 2023, the number of laws utilized to prosecute individuals openly participating in contentious events opposing the Russian invasion surged. The most frequently invoked law against participants across the country was the newly instituted article on public dissemination of knowingly false information regarding the military, state authorities, and affiliated actors and individuals.

In 2023, contention continued to decline. To express their disagreement with the regime, claim-makers continued to hold individual pickets and erect monuments to commemorate victims of the war and repression, often facing detainees and assault from the police. The officials refused to approve a Nemtsov rally on February 27, but some individuals brought flowers to the politician's memorial on the bridge where he was murdered. Similar commemorative events took place around the country in other major cities.

4.4.4 Regional Contention in 2020–2023

Throughout the period, all eight clusters witnessed a significant decline in events. Most contention occurred in Moscow, Khabarovsk Krai, Saint Petersburg, Sverdlovsk Oblast, Novosibirsk Oblast, and Moscow Oblast, with Moscow alone reporting more than 1,000 instances of contentious action. The prevailing trends of contention in 2020–2021 were echoed across most clusters, indicative of the number of rallies organized nationwide, primarily arranged by countrywide organizations with a regional presence (Figure 15). The median number of events showed a downward trend in most clusters, with no significant diversity in contentious events. The reduction in contention started in March 2022, following the Russian invasion of Ukraine on February 24.

The most remarkable change occurred with the contentious events in Khabarovsk, where support for the Krai's governor was demonstrated through rallies held for several months until further dispersal, thereby marking it as one of the most contentious regions during the period. Another significant outlier was North Ossetia, which experienced substantial contentious action against COVID-19 measures. This contentious action was violently suppressed, with no subsequent backlash.

Another notable development was shown in Chechnya, where mothers of mobilized soldiers and men held rallies to ask the head of the republic and

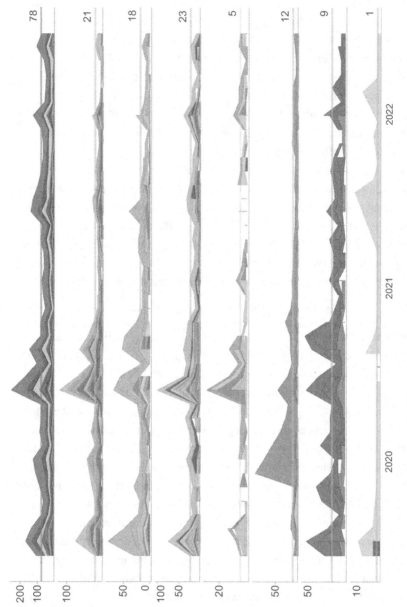

Figure 15 A comparison of contentious trends distributed among the eight clusters in 2020–2023.

the federal government not to mobilize Chechen men for the war in Ukraine. In response, Kadyrov announced that mobilization would not be held in the republic since the region had already supplied enough soldiers and had enough people willing to commit themselves and volunteer for war.

All clusters showed a decline in various types of events that had been present throughout the 2011–2015 and 2016–2019 periods, including environmental, labor, and other issue-specific demonstrations, thereby showcasing the regime's zero tolerance toward any gatherings, especially after the invasion. Commemorative rallies and pro-government events were still held during this period, especially those in support of the war.

The average number of contentious events decreased across all clusters nationwide. Although some regions experienced developments tied to local politics, the majority mirrored the patterns of contention observed in the main clusters. It suggests a presence of countrywide activities, albeit lacking local structures for organized contentious action.

4.4.5 Authoritarian Innovation and Contention in 2020–2023: Some Conclusions

The period from 2020 to 2023 witnessed escalated repression aimed at political organizations and individuals who opposed the regime or expressed public disagreement with politics. The heightened repression manifested through increased instances of violence, reactive measures, political persecution on various pretexts, and elevated fines, arrests, and imprisonments. These tactics encompassed all the repressive strategies introduced over previous years and were amplified in terms of force and violence and supplemented by further innovative strategies, as listed in Table 9. By 2023, the landscape of contentious action had significantly changed in terms of incidence and repertoires. Environmental, labor, and other issue-specific events almost disappeared, alongside a general decline in other forms of political participation, especially following the full-scale invasion.

The regime successfully deterred individuals from engaging in contentious action, particularly following the full-scale invasion of Ukraine. By demonstrating zero tolerance toward contention, the regime minimized all forms of public participation and punished those who sought to challenge its stance even in the absence of any evident activities. Notably, detentions surpassed the instances of contention, indicating a surge in repressive measures.

The inability to participate in or obtain permission for organized events led to individual picketing. However, this was classified as a mass event, leading to multiple detentions. Following the suppressive measures and detentions carried out in Russia during February and March, contentious events in general saw a

Table 9 Repressive strategies employed by the state in 2020–2023 redefined according to changes implemented by the state if compared to 2011–2015 and 2016–2019

Repression	Strategy	Definition
Reactive repression	Detentions	Detentions prior to or during contention followed by arrests and legal action, including individual picketing
	Barriers, zoning, and dispersal techniques	Obstacles and tactics to encircle, divide, and disperse or prevent protesters from entering particular areas.
	Violence	Physical damage, torture, beatings, the use of tear gas, batons, electroshock weapons, and other equipment; denial of medical assistance in case of heavy injuries.
	Blocked internet access	Blocked access to internet and cellular services
Proactive repression	Event authorization	Discretionary rejection of applications and increasing requirements to gain authorization, including restrictions on location; withdrawal of existing authorization
	Repressive legislation	New legislation imposing more restrictions on participation and expression
	Criminalization of participation	Repeated participation in contentious events classified as a criminal offense and results in prison sentence
	Political persecution	Politically motivated judicial persecution with procedural violations
	Foreign agent legislation	The use of foreign agent legislation against organizations and individuals to limit their professional activities and activism
	Police raids and extended authority	Police raids and searches targeted at individuals or organizations for intimidation or further persecution; extended authority to access people's property

Heightened security measures	Increased police presence and blocked public access to specific locations
Threats and intimidation	Threats and intimidation to deter participation; employment retaliation
Pro-government events	Events arranged by the state using coercion or monetary incentives for participants
Media blackouts	Intentionally underreporting contentious events; publishing false information about contentious events and the opposition
Website blocklists	Blockage of independent media and social platforms
Digital surveillance	Monitoring of online expression, arresting and sentencing violators
Facial recognition	The use of facial recognition system to detain potential or previous event participants

decline. Individuals who made online posts criticizing the regime were also detained.

There was a noticeable decline in the average number of contentious events. The regime imposed stringent restrictions on mass gatherings and rallies and actively repressed various contentious activities nationwide. Furthermore, many repressive measures were employed: activists were imprisoned, leaders were persecuted, and concerted efforts were made to dismantle existing organizations and individuals previously engaged in organizing contentious events. One prominent target was the Anticorruption Foundation, with its leader Navalny enduring poisoning and subsequent imprisonment.

Innovative strategies included using facial recognition systems to spot and detain participants before or after unauthorized gatherings. Random detentions occurred among individuals who did not participate in the events but allegedly wore signs and colors that could be interpreted as support for Ukraine. Moreover, there was a significant increase in cases related to expressing political views online and further persecution for providing so-called fake information about the regime, its past, and current operations, including government officials. The regime utilized foreign agent legislation against individuals, thereby declaring some activists and critics as foreign agents. Preceded by an extended definition of what constitutes a foreign agent, these measures imposed limitations on activities such as participation in elections, engaging with the media, delivering public lectures, and holding particular positions. This utilization of the foreign agent legislation became a tool for persecution and limiting access to political resources, forcing individuals to either leave the country, cease public activities, or potentially face further persecution. These actions reduced the capacity of public figures and the opposition to mobilize support.

The regime introduced new legislation to politically persecute individuals, as shown in Table 10. The spectrum of laws utilized against citizens evolved significantly, reducing reliance on extremist and terrorist legislation while broadening the scope of possible violations. The most frequently used legislation charged individuals for expressing themselves or disseminating information deemed by the regime as false and undermining it in any way. This classification is suited for persecuting individuals who openly oppose state actors, especially the Armed Forces, during contentious events. Another important consideration is the explicit portrayal of the internet as a tool that, when used to express political views opposing the regime, resulted in criminal investigations, hefty fines, and possible imprisonment for repeat violations. A few provisions, such as the article on vandalism and intentional destruction of

Table 10 Political persecutions against individuals during 2020–2023 by
Article from the Criminal Code

Article	Description	Count
207.3 Part 2	Public dissemination of knowingly false information about the military, state authorities, and affiliated bodies done by officials or groups to profit or express enmity	99
205.2 Part 2	Public propaganda, justification, or calls for terrorism using the internet	91
280.3 Part 1	Public actions discrediting the armed forces	86
318 Part 1	Use of violence against a public official or threats	86
214 Part 2	Group vandalism on the grounds of hatred or enmity	63
207.3 Part 1	Public dissemination of knowingly false information about the military, state officials, and affiliated bodies	52
282.2 Part 1	Organization of the activity of an extremist organization	50
282.2 Part 2	Participation in an extremist organization after its legal liquidation or ban	46
280 Part 2	Public calls for extremism using the internet	36
30 Part 1	Preparations to commit a crime	30
167 Part 2	Intentional property damage or destruction causing severe consequences	29
207 Part 2	Knowingly false reporting on an act of terrorism	27
267 Part 1	Destruction of or damaging of transport vehicles or communication routes	26
282 Part 2	Actions to incite hatred or enmity using mass media or the internet	26
236 Part 2	Violation of sanitary-epidemiological rules caused the death of an individual	25

Source: Federal Protective Service of the Russian Federation (2023); OVD-Info (2023a)

property, emerged in response to graffiti and writings on the walls of buildings, including government buildings. This reflects the increasing incidence of such violations, particularly following the onset of the war.

5 Conclusion

5.1 The Regime and Contention in Russia

As the political regime in Russia evolved, it relied on proactive and reactive repressive strategies to deter citizens from making political claims against the regime. Through engaging in tactical innovation against claim-makers, the Kremlin successfully altered the repertoires of contentious action. The case of Russia suggests that tactical interactions – innovative responses and counterresponses between the regime and its opponents, as McAdam (1983) defined – play a critical role. In tracing the evolution of regime strategies in Russia, it is evident that the regime introduced proactive repression not only in response to existing contentious action but also preemptively during periods of reduced contention. Initially, the regime avoided overt violence, indicating that actions undertaken by the authorities were not always in tactical response to contention or, in line with Ritter and Conrad (2016), did not necessarily lead to direct repression, particularly when contentious action was held within expected repertoires.

Russia's regime exemplifies the adaptability of authoritarian regimes in implementing novel approaches to repression. Similar to observations from protest studies in the United States, the regime did not always generate novel tactics, but its innovation emerged from the strategic combination of tactics previously utilized by the regime (Wang & Soule, 2016). Through reliance on foreign agent, NGO, and anti-extremism legislation, the Russian regime leveraged these laws to politically persecute its opponents throughout the 2010s. In the 2020s, while newer legislation – such as COVID-19 restrictions and war-related legislation – was employed more frequently, the regime had also increasingly imposed heavier sanctions on violators of the extremism laws. Additionally, it introduced and experimented with other legal measures such as incarceration for repetitive violations, higher fines, and administrative detentions to many existing regulations, demonstrating a continued evolution in already existing legislation as the regime increasingly infringed on civil liberties and authoritarianism continued to rise.

The findings of this study also challenge the assertion that modern authoritarian regimes may favor nonviolence and are inclined to utilize sophisticated preventive measures alongside it. As Moss (2014) argued, while modern authoritarian regimes may present a facade of liberalism – a trend nevertheless observable in the 2012–2015 and 2016–2019 periods – the evolution of authoritarianism in Russia from 2011 to 2023 saw the regime bolstering its police and internal military forces, augmenting their power and authority to use force against protesters. Proactive strategies employed by the regime largely relied on the methods of political persecution and intimidation, while the number of political prisoners increased exponentially and the instances of contention continued to decline. This finding underscores that covert repression might not always be the preferred strategy of political regimes and it also hints at the potential adaptability and escalation of repression tactics by regime over time. In line with Curato and Fossati (2020), Wang and Soule (2016), and Pepinsky (2020), the increase in violence can be defined as a novel tool in the current regime setting and a measure deemed necessary to ensure regime longevity and potentially prevent dissent. The mimicry of democracy does not inherently deter a regime from resorting to violence; rather, violence may be strategically employed if perceived as efficient.

That being said, the regime incorporated methods that did not involve direct violence or coercion that served as deterrence. During 2011–2012, it allowed contentious events to occur without resorting to violence or imprisoning participants, exploring indirect means to deter citizens from participating instead. As Tertytchnaya (2023) points out, one of the critical mechanisms employed by the regime to reduce participation was the authorization of mass events. Initially presented as a tool for negotiation and ensuring that the officials could accommodate requirements and provide necessary arrangements for citizens to express themselves peacefully, it served as a mechanism to control the number and locations of events. Faced with refusals, event organizers often chose not to initiate conflict to avoid placing participants in danger of detention or repression for participating in an unauthorized event, at the very least.

The use of this additional preventative strategy allowed the regime to sanction claim-makers who did not comply with the requirement, potentially facilitating more detention and violence. As the officials increased the rate of refusals for authorization, organizers decided to hold unauthorized events, which faced greater scrutiny and a larger presence of law enforcement officers. As unauthorized contention became more frequent, the regime attempted to discredit the participants, intimidate the organizers, and deter people from making political claims by detaining or intimidating them. In addition to these reactive measures, the regime imposed heavier punishment on participants and organizers by increasing fines and arrests. Law enforcement officers were not hesitant to employ repression against claim-makers and critics who held events despite the denial of authorization.

It is problematic to measure precisely how each innovative strategy introduced over this period altered contention due to their complexity and constant evolution. Nonetheless, authoritarian innovation in Russia should be seen as a constantly evolving mechanism complicated by a large set of tools and approaches that complement each other. Whenever detentions and violence are insufficient, the regime targets organizational structures and influential individuals who act as integral parts of these structures. Whenever critics of the regime and its policies emerge, their access is restricted through political persecution or by employing foreign agent legislation that prevents them from engaging in particular activities. If violence is employed or a citizen attempts to use any kind of physical force against an official, they face severe sanctions, as do their associates or people present at the same event. Legislative acts enacted in 2012–2015 and 2016–2020 laid a foundation to restrict citizens from disseminating information that contradicts or discredits the regime in 2020–2023.

In an effort to position itself as an alternative to the repressive regime, the opposition explicitly refrained from resorting to violence against the state and law enforcement. Despite the increase in contentious action, the opposition continued its repertoires of contention revolving around rallies, demonstrations, and marches. Even when the regime used force, no backlash occurred. Contentious events were confined to specific dates, rarely being continuous or spontaneous, which enabled the regime to prepare and coordinate its response among different bodies involved in contentious politics. Through authoritarian innovation, the regime ensured its capacity to repress and the ability to preempt or address any changes in contentious repertoires of the opposition.

Despite attempts to organize contentious events nationwide through the presence of local representatives and offices of the opposition bodies, the most significant rallies occurred in specific regional clusters. At the same time, some regions saw no participation and did not engage in contention. Thus, despite significant demonstrations in Ingushetia or Khabarovsk, regions generally aligned with the main events organized by opposition bodies, with Moscow and Saint Petersburg remaining the central hubs of contention. Local social movements and organizations were either banned by authorities or had limited support, thus being merely auxiliary to the main events unfolding in a handful of regions. Whenever necessary, the regime exercised its force by deploying Rosgvardia officers from neighboring regions to disperse crowds and persecuted activists outside of their home region, as evidenced in the case of Ingushetia.

5.2 Beyond Russian Repression

Drawing from the literature on contentious politics, political participation, political regime classification, authoritarianism, repression, and authoritarian innovation, and using the example of Russia, one of the modern repressive authoritarian regimes, this Element examines how authoritarianism shapes contentious action through innovative repression strategies over time. It emphasizes the importance of repression as an attribute of authoritarianism and focuses on violations of civil liberties, analyzing how regimes can alter contentious action short- and long term. This research also explores how initially sophisticated methods of covert repression may combine and evolve into innovative strategies previously absent in contentious politics, enabling the regime to control how people protest and to impose threats on claim-makers increasing their costs of political participation.

Rather than focusing on the innovation employed by claim-makers and its influence on repression, this Element offers a more regime-centric perspective where the regime acts as the initiator of innovative strategies aimed at ensuring longevity. This approach diverges from the opposition-centric perspective prevalent in studies of contentious politics in democracies, which posits that regime opponents structure contentious action through their responses to threats from the regime and their ability to innovate within the existing repertoires of contention. Through a detailed examination of the methods employed by the regime over time, this research provides an overview of how repertoires of contentious action were transformed and assesses the impact of the regime's broader strategy on this transformation, achieved through both proactive and reactive methods of repression.

By analyzing how a specific regime infringes upon civil liberties through its authoritarian institutions, I identify particular strategies the regime employed and observe how these strategies shaped political participation. Using this approach, this Element bridges the field of contention and authoritarian politics, exploring how particular decisions either facilitate or deter contentious action over longer periods to ensure longevity.

Using novel computational techniques, this Element presents a methodological workflow that facilitates the data collection process for analyzing protests in authoritarian regimes. Employing the advancements of machine learning, I demonstrate how these computational techniques could be effectively utilized in protest event analysis to automate the process and significantly reduce the time-consuming and resource-intensive tasks associated with manual coding.

While this research primarily focuses on proactive and reactive repression as key determinants of a political regime type and contention, it also acknowledges that other attributes, such as cooptation and legitimation, also play a crucial role in contentious politics. Future research could also benefit from more detailed investigations into specific instances of contention, examining interactions both within the polity and the opposition. Exploring how these dynamics evolve through innovative interactions between the regime and its opponents could provide valuable insights into how contentious repertoires develop over time.

This analysis, being focused on a single case study, has its limitations. Future studies could engage in the broader discussion on how authoritarian regimes innovate by examining a wider range of such regimes through a comparative perspective. It would contribute to the understanding of how they learn from each other, which strategies are most effective in shaping contention, and how they develop their repressive strategies over time. Additionally, it would enable a deeper understanding of how specific decisions made by these regimes impact protest, and how political participation and contentious politics are being transformed in the context of increasingly complex repression.

Investigating processes across different regimes, including how democracies innovate in repression and how these innovations are adopted by or from authoritarian regimes, could also be an important contribution to learning more about such phenomena as democratic backsliding and contentious action. More analysis is needed to examine how specific policies lead to varied outcomes across different regime types, with broader implications for policymaking.

Future research should also explore the motivations behind regimes' adoption of particular preventive strategies. These strategies may not always directly respond to actions by regime opponents but could be implemented ad hoc, even in the absence of any immediate threat from actors within the regime. The concept of authoritarian learning offers valuable insights, suggesting that regimes might select innovative tactics based on observed threats in other regimes, through trial and error within their political systems, or their unique contexts.

References

Adamson, F. B. (2020). Non-state authoritarianism and diaspora politics. *Global Networks*, *20*(1), 150–169.

Alexanyan, K., Barash, V., Etling, B., et al. (2012). Exploring Russian cyberspace: Digitally-mediated collective action and the networked public sphere. *Berkman Center Research Publication*, (2).

Alieva, I., Moffitt, J., & Carley, K. M. (2022). How disinformation operations against Russian opposition leader Alexei Navalny influence the international audience on Twitter. *Social Network Analysis and Mining*, *12*(1), 80.

Almeida, P. (2003). Opportunity organizations and threat-induced contention: Protest waves in authoritarian settings. *American Journal of Sociology*, *109*(2), 345–400.

Alvarez, M., Cheibub, J. A., Limongi, F., & Przeworski, A. (1996). Classifying political regimes. *Studies in Comparative International Development*, *31*, 3–36.

Amnesty International. (2012). *The circle of injustice: Security operations and human rights violations in Ingushetia* (Tech. Rep.). www.amnesty.org/en/documents/eur46/005/2012/en/

Anckar, C., & Fredriksson, C. (2019). Classifying political regimes 1800–2016: A typology and a new dataset. *European Political Science*, *18*(1), 84–96.

Arslanalp, M., & Erkmen, T. D. (2020). Mobile emergency rule in Turkey: Legal repression of protests during authoritarian transformation. *Democratization*, *27*(6), 947–969.

Ash, K. (2015). The election trap: The cycle of post-electoral repression and opposition fragmentation in Lukashenko's Belarus. *Democratization*, *22*(6), 1030–1053.

Azhgikhina, N. (2007). The struggle for press freedom in Russia: Reflections of a Russian journalist. *Europe-Asia Studies*, *59*(8), 1245–1262.

Bader, M., Enikolopov, R., Petrova, M., & Sonin, K. (2014). Fraud and elections in authoritarian regimes: Evidence from a field experiment in Russia. *American Political Science Review*, *108*(1), 144–158.

BBC News. (2016, November 1). *Russia activist Ildar Dadin accuses prison of torture.* https://www.bbc.com/news/world-europe-37836739

Biggs, M. (2015). Has protest increased since the 1970s? How a survey question can construct a spurious trend. *British Journal of Sociology*, *66*(1), 141–62.

Biggs, M. (2018). Size matters: Quantifying protest by counting participants. *Sociological Methods & Research, 47*(3), 351–383.

Bjørnskov, C., & Rode, M. (2019). Regime types and regime change: A new dataset on democracy, coups, and political institutions. *The Review of International Organizations, 15*(2), 531–551.

Bjørnskov, C., & Rode, M. (2020). Regime types and regime change: A new dataset on democracy, coups, and political institutions. *The Review of International Organizations, 15*, 531–551.

Bodrunova, S. S., Litvinenko, A., & Nigmatullina, K. (2021). Who is the censor? Self-censorship of Russian journalists in professional routines and social networking. *Journalism, 22*(12), 2919–2937.

Boon, K. M. (2022). 'The only thing is you have to know them first': Protest policing and Malaysia's BERSIH protests (2011–2016). *Small Wars & Insurgencies, 33*(4–5), 868–901.

Boutros, M. (2017). Place and tactical innovation in social movements: The emergence of Egypt's anti-harassment groups. *Theory and Society, 46*, 543–575.

Breuer, A., Landman, T., & Farquhar, D. (2015). Social media and protest mobilization: Evidence from the Tunisian revolution. *Democratization, 22*(4), 764–792.

Buitinck, L., Louppe, G., Blondel, M., et al. (2013). API design for machine learning software: Experiences from the scikit-learn project. *arXiv preprint arXiv:1309.0238.*

Burtsev, M., Seliverstov, A., Airapetyan, R., et al. (2018). Deeppavlov: Open-source library for dialogue systems. In *Proceedings of ACL 2018, system demonstrations* (pp. 122–127).

Carles, B., Miller, M., & Sebastian, R. (2018). *Boix-miller-rosato dichotomous coding of democracy, 1800–2015.* Harvard Dataverse.

Centre, M. H. R. (2013). *The case of Gelendghik human rights activists.* https://memohrc.org/ru/special-projects/delo-gelendzhikskih-pravozashchitnikov

Cha, M., Haddadi, H., Benevenuto, F., & Gummadi, K. (2010). Measuring user influence in Twitter: The million follower fallacy. In *Proceedings of the international AAAI conference on web and social media* (Vol. 4, pp. 10–17).

Chaisty, P., & Whitefield, S. (2013). Forward to democracy or back to authoritarianism? The attitudinal bases of mass support for the Russian election protests of 2011–2012. *Post-Soviet Affairs, 29*(5), 387–403.

Chau, T.- H., & Wan, K.- M. (2024). Pour (tear) gas on fire? Violent confrontations and anti-government backlash. *Political Science Research and Methods, 12*(1), 184–194.

Chen, X., & Moss, D. M. (2018). Authoritarian regimes and social movements. In D. A. Snow, S. A. Soule, H. Kriesi, & H. J. McCammon (Eds.), *The Wiley Blackwell companion to social movements* (pp. 666–681). Chichester: John Wiley & Sons.

Cheskin, A., & March, L. (2015). State-society relations in contemporary Russia: New forms of political and social contention. *East European Politics, 31*(3), 261–273.

Coppedge, M., Lindberg, S., Skaaning, S. E., & Teorell, J. (2016). Measuring high-level democratic principles using the v-dem data. *International Political Science Review, 37*(5), 580–593.

Corduneanu-Huci, C., & Osa, M. (2003). Running uphill: Political opportunity in non-democracies. *Comparative Sociology, 2*(4), 605–629.

Crossley, N. (2002). Repertoires of contention and tactical diversity in the UK psychiatric survivors movement: The question of appropriation. *Social Movement Studies, 1*(1), 47–71.

Curato, N., & Fossati, D. (2020). Authoritarian innovations: Crafting support for a less democratic Southeast Asia. *Democratization, 27*(6), 1006–1020.

Dahl, R. (1971). *Polyarchy. Participation and Opposition.* New Haven: Yale University Press.

Daucé, F. (2014). The government and human rights groups in Russia: Civilized oppression? *Journal of Civil Society, 10*(3), 239–254.

Davenport, C. (1995). Multi-dimensional threat perception and state repression: An inquiry into why states apply negative sanctions. *American Journal of Political Science*, 683–713.

Dehghan, E., & Glazunova, S. (2021). "Fake news" discourses: An exploration of Russian and Persian tweets. *Journal of Language and Politics, 20*(5), 741–760.

della Porta, D. (2011). Eventful protest, global conflicts. *Distinktion: Journal of Social Theory. 9*(2), 27–56.

Devlin, J., Chang, M.- W., Lee, K., & Toutanova, K. (2018). BERT: Pre-training of deep bidirectional transformers for language understanding. *arXiv preprint arXiv:1810.04805.*

Dollbaum, J. M. (2021a). Protest event analysis under conditions of limited press freedom: Comparing data sources. *Media and Communication, 9*(4), 104–115.

Dollbaum, J. M. (2021b). Social policy on social media: How opposition actors used Twitter and VKontakte to oppose the Russian pension reform. *Problems of Post-Communism, 68*(6), 509–520.

Earl, J. (2003). Tanks, tear gas, and taxes: Toward a theory of movement repression. *Sociological Theory, 21*(1), 44–68.

Earl, J. (2011). Political repression: Iron fists, velvet gloves, and diffuse control. *Annual Review of Sociology, 37*, 261–284.

Edwards, G. (2016). In N. Crossley & J. Krinsky (Eds.), *Social networks and social movements* (pp. 48–69). Routledge.

Eisinger, P. K. (1973). The conditions of protest behavior in American cities. *American Political Science Review. 67*(1), 11–28.

Enikolopov, R., Korovkin, V., Petrova, M., Sonin, K., & Zakharov, A. V. (2012). Field experiment estimate of electoral fraud in Russian parliamentary elections. *Proceedings of the National Academy of Sciences.*

Esen, B., & Gumuscu, S. (2016). Rising competitive authoritarianism in Turkey. *Third World Quarterly, 37*(9), 1581–1606.

Federal Assembly of the Russian Federation. (2004). *Federal Law of June 19, 2004 No. 54-FZ.*

Federal Assembly of the Russian Federation. (2022). *Article 20.2 of Code of Administrative Offences* [Government Document].

Federal Assembly of the Russian Federation. (2023a). *Administrative Code of the Russian Federation.*

Federal Assembly of the Russian Federation. (2023b). *Article 20.2 of the Administrative Code of the Russian Federation.*

Federal Assembly of the Russian Federation. (2023c). *Criminal Code of the Russian Federation.*

Federal Protective Service of the Russian Federation. (2023). *Official internet portal of legal information.* http://pravo.gov.ru/

FIDH. (2018). *Russia 2012–2018: 50 anti-democracy laws entered into force within last presidential mandate.* www.fidh.org/en/region/europe-central-asia/russia/russia-2012-2018-50-anti-democracy-laws-entered-into-force-within

FIDH. (2023). *FIDH documents the destruction of civil society in Russia, law after law.* www.fidh.org/en/region/europe-central-asia/russia/fidh-docu ments-the-destruction-of-civil-society-in-russia-law-after

Ford, M., Gillan, M., & Ward, K. (2021). Authoritarian innovations in labor governance: The case of Cambodia. *Governance, 34*(4), 1255–1271.

Freedom House. (2023). *Marking 50 years in the struggle for democracy* (Report). Freedom House. https://freedomhouse.org/report/freedom-world/2023/marking-50-years

Gabdulhakov, R. (2020). (Con)trolling the web: Social media user arrests, state-supported vigilantism and citizen counter-forces in Russia. *Global Crime, 21*(3–4), 283–305.

Gabowitsch, M. (2018). Are copycats subversive? Strategy-31, the Russian runs, the immortal regiment, and the transformative potential of non-hierarchical movements. *Problems of Post-Communism, 65*(5), 297–314.

Galeotti, M. (2021). The silovik-industrial complex: Russia's national guard as coercive, political, economic and cultural force. *Demokratizatsiya: The Journal of Post-Soviet Democratization, 29*(1), 3–29.

Gandhi, J., & Przeworski, A. (2007). Authoritarian institutions and the survival of autocrats. *Comparative Political Studies, 40*(11), 1279–1301.

Gel'man, V. (2016). The politics of fear: How Russia's rulers counter their rivals. *Russian Politics, 1*(1), 27–45.

Glasius, M. (2018). What authoritarianism is … and is not: A practice perspective. *International Affairs, 94*(3), 515–533.

Göbel, C. (2021). The political logic of protest repression in China. *Journal of Contemporary China, 30*(128), 169–185.

Goldstone, J. (2016). Protest and repression in democracies and autocracies: Europe, Iran, Thailand and the Middle East 2010–11. In S. Seferiades & H. Johnston (Eds.), Violent protest, contentious politics, and the neoliberal state (p. 103–117). Routledge.

Goldstone, J., & Tilly, C. (2001). Threat (and opportunity): Popular action and state response in the dynamics of contentious action. *Silence and Voice in the Study of Contentious Politics*, 179–194.

Grießhaber, D., Maucher, J., & Vu, N. T. (2020). Fine-tuning BERT for low-resource natural language understanding via active learning. *arXiv preprint arXiv:2012.02462.*

Grimm, J., & Harders, C. (2018). Unpacking the effects of repression: The evolution of Islamist repertoires of contention in Egypt after the fall of president Morsi. *Social Movement Studies, 17*(1), 1–18.

Gupta, D. K., Singh, H., & Sprague, T. (1993). Government coercion of dissidents: Deterrence or provocation? *Journal of Conflict Resolution, 37*(2), 301–339.

Guriev, S., & Treisman, D. (2020). A theory of informational autocracy. *Journal of Public Economics, 186*, 104158.

Hall, S. G., & Ambrosio, T. (2017). Authoritarian learning: A conceptual overview. *East European Politics, 33*(2), 143–161.

Hassanpour, N. (2014). Media disruption and revolutionary unrest: Evidence from Mubarak's quasi-experiment. *Political Communication, 31*(1), 1–24.

Hellmeier, S., & Weidmann, N. B. (2020). Pulling the strings? The strategic use of pro-government mobilization in authoritarian regimes. *Comparative Political Studies, 53*(1), 71–108.

Heydemann, S. (2013). Tracking the Arab Spring: Syria and the future of authoritarianism. *Journal of Democracy, 24*(4), 59–73.

Heydemann, S., & Leenders, R. (2011). Authoritarian learning and authoritarian resilience: Regime responses to the "Arab Awakening." *Globalizations, 8*(5), 647–653.

Heydemann, S., & Leenders, R. (2014). Authoritarian learning and counterrevolution. In M. Lynch (ed.), *The Arab uprisings explained: New contentious politics in the middle east* (pp. 75–92). Columbia University Press.

Horvath, R. (2011). Putin's "preventive counter-revolution": Post-soviet authoritarianism and the spectre of velvet revolution. *Europe-Asia Studies, 63*(1), 1–25.

Human Rights Watch. (2008). *World report 2008: Russia.* www.hrw.org/world-report/2008/country-chapters-6

Jay Chen, C.- J. (2020). A protest society evaluated: Popular protests in China, 2000–2019. *Mobilization: An International Quarterly, 25*(SI), 641–660.

Judicial Department of the Supreme Court. (2023). *Report on the work of courts of general jurisdiction in considering cases of administrative offences.* www.cdep.ru/index.php?id=79&item=3417.

Khovalyg, D. (2023). On "New Tuva" anti-war movement. *Inner Asia, 25*(1), 118–125.

Kriesi, H., Hutter, S., & Bojar, A. (2019). Contentious episode analysis. *Mobilization: An International Quarterly, 24*(3), 251–273.

Kuratov, Y., & Arkhipov, M. (2019). Adaptation of deep bidirectional multilingual transformers for Russian Language. *Computing Research Repository.* http://arxiv.org/abs/1905.07213.

Lang, B. (2018). Authoritarian learning in china's civil society regulations: Towards a multi-level framework. *Journal of Current Chinese Affairs, 47*(3), 147–186.

Lankina, T. (2015). The dynamics of regional and national contentious politics in Russia: Evidence from a new dataset. *Problems of Post-Communism, 62*(1), 26–44.

LaPorte, J. (2015). Hidden in plain sight: Political opposition and hegemonic authoritarianism in Azerbaijan. *Post-Soviet Affairs, 31*(4), 339–366.

Levitsky, S., & Way, L. A. (2002). Elections without democracy: The rise of competitive authoritarianism. *Journal of Democracy, 13*(2), 51–65.

Levitsky, S., & Way, L. A. (2010). *Competitive authoritarianism: Hybrid regimes after the cold war.* Cambridge University Press.

Libman, A. (2017). Subnational political regimes and formal economic regulation: Evidence from Russian regions. *Regional & Federal Studies, 27*(2), 127–151.

Lichbach, M. I. (1987). Deterrence or escalation?: The puzzle of aggregate studies of repression and dissent. *Journal of Conflict Resolution, 31*(2), 266–297.

Lipman, M. (2010). Freedom of expression without freedom of the press. *Journal of International Affairs, 63*(2), 153–169.

Lipsky, M. (1968). Protest as a political resources. *American Political Science Review, 62*(4), 1144–1158.

Loshchilov, I., & Hutter, F. (2017). Decoupled weight decay regularization. *arXiv preprint arXiv:1711.05101*.

Loveman, M. (1998). High-risk collective action: Defending human rights in Chile, Uruguay, and Argentina. *American Journal of Sociology, 104*(2), 477–525.

Lührmann, A., Tannenberg, M., & Lindberg, S. I. (2018). Regimes of the world (row): Opening new avenues for the comparative study of political regimes. *Politics and Governance, 6*(1), 60–77.

Maddi, S. R., Harvey, R. H., Khoshaba, D. M., et al. (2006). The personality construct of hardiness, iii: Relationships with repression, innovativeness, authoritarianism, and performance. *Journal of Personality, 74*(2), 575–598.

Magaloni, B., Chu, J., & Min, E. (2013). *Autocracies of the world, 1950–2012 (version 1.0)*. Dataset, Stanford University.

Mapes, N., White, A., Medury, R., & Dua, S. (2019). Divisive language and propaganda detection using multi-head attention transformers with deep learning BERT-based language models for binary classification. In *Proceedings of the second workshop on natural language processing for internet freedom: Censorship, disinformation, and propaganda* (p. 103–106).

Marshall, M. G., Jaggers, K., & Gurr, T. R. (2010). Polity iv project: Political regime characteristics and transitions, 1800–2010. *Center for Systemic Peace, 10*, 24–37.

Marty, D. (2009). *Situation in the North Caucasus region: security and human rights* (Tech. Rep.). Committee on Legal Affairs and Human Rights, Parliamentary Assembly of the Council of Europe. http://assembly.coe.int/CommitteeDocs/2009/ajdoc43_2009.pdf

McAdam, D. (1983). Tactical innovation and the pace of insurgency. *American Sociological Review, 48*(6), 735–754.

McAdam, D., & Tarrow, S. (2018). The political context of social movements. In D. A. Snow, S. A. Soule, H. Kriesi, & H. J. McCammon (Eds.), *The Wiley Blackwell companion to social movements* (pp. 17–42). John Wiley & Sons.

McAdam, D., Tarrow, S., & Tilly, C. (2012). *Dynamics of contention*. Cambridge University Press.

McCarthy, J. D., & Zald, M. N. (1977). Resource mobilization and social movements: A partial theory. *American Journal of Sociology*, *82*(6), 1212–1241.

McCarthy, L. A., Rice, D., & Lokhmutov, A. (2023). Four months of "discrediting the military": Repressive law in wartime Russia. *Demokratizatsiya: The Journal of Post-Soviet Democratization*, *31*(2), 125–160.

Meyer, D. (2004). Protest and political opportunities. *Annual Review of Sociology*, *30*, 125–145.

Mietzner, M. (2020). Authoritarian innovations in Indonesia: Electoral narrowing, identity politics and executive illiberalism. *Democratization*, *27*(6), 1021–1036.

Moore, W. H. (1998). Repression and dissent: Substitution, context, and timing. *American Journal of Political Science*, *42*(3), 851–873.

Morgenbesser, L. (2020a). The menu of autocratic innovation. *Democratization*, *27*(6), 1053–1072.

Morgenbesser, L. (2020b). *The rise of sophisticated authoritarianism in Southeast Asia*. Cambridge University Press.

Morris, A. D. (1984). *The origins of the civil rights movement*. Simon and Schuster.

Moss, D. (2014). Repression, response, and contained escalation under "liberalized" authoritarianism in Jordan. *Mobilization: An International Quarterly*, *19*(3), 261–286.

Munck, G. L., & Verkuilen, J. (2002). Conceptualizing and measuring democracy - evaluating alternative indices. *Comparative Political Studies*, *35*(1), 5–34.

Mustafa, B. (2023). Post-tishreen online feminism: Continuity, rupture, departure. *International Journal of Middle East Studies*, *55*(2), 328–335.

Nicholson, M. (2020). *Towards a Russia of the regions*. Routledge.

Norén-Nilsson, A. (2021). Fresh news, innovative news: Popularizing Cambodia's authoritarian turn. *Critical Asian Studies*, *53*(1), 89–108.

Novaya Gazeta. (2021). The Ingush case of Russia. *Novaya Gazeta*. https://novayagazeta.ru/articles/2021/05/13/ingushskoe-delo-rossii

Omelicheva, M. Y. (2021). *Repression trap: The mechanism of escalating state violence in Russia* (Tech. Rep.). Center for Strategic and International Studies (CSIS).

Ong, L. H., & Han, D. (2019). What drives people to protest in an authoritarian country? Resources and rewards vs risks of protests in urban and rural China. *Political Studies*, *67*(1), 224–248.

Opp, K. (2022). *Advanced introduction to social movements and political protests*. Edward Elgar.

Opp, K.- D. (1994). Repression and revolutionary action: East Germany in 1989. *Rationality and Society, 6*(1), 101–138.

Opp, K.- D. (2009). *Theories of political protest and social movements: A multidisciplinary introduction, critique, and synthesis.* New York: Routledge.

Ortmann, S. (2023). When protests become a threat to authoritarian rule: The case of environmental protests in Viet Nam. *Third World Quarterly, 44*(9), 2063–2079.

Ortmann, S., & Thompson, M. R. (2020). *China's "Singapore model" and authoritarian learning.* Routledge.

Osa, M., & Schock, K. (2007). A long, hard slog: Political opportunities, social networks and the mobilization of dissent in non-democracies. In G. C. Patrick (Ed.), *Research in social movements, conflicts and change* (Vol. 27, pp. 123–153). Emerald Group.

OVD-Info. (2014). *Political repressions in Russia in 2011–2014: Criminal prosecutions.* https://reports.ovdinfo.org/2014/cr-report/

OVD-Info. (2018, October 27). *The "New Greatness" case: Who are these people, and why are they being tried? An OVD-Info guide.* https://ovd.info/articles/2018/10/27/delo-novogo-velichiya-kto-eti-lyudi-i-za-chto-ih-sudyat-gid-ovd-info

OVD-Info. (2019, May 13). *The "Network" case: Who are these people, and why are they being tried? An OVD-Info guide.* https://ovd.info/articles/2019/05/13/delo-seti-kto-eti-lyudi-i-za-chto-ih-sudyat-gid-ovd-info

OVD-Info. (2023a, July 17). *Database of politically motivated criminal prosecutions.* https://data.ovd.info/politpressing

OVD-Info. (2023b). *20.2 administrative offenses code: Application.* https://data-scripts.ovd.info/20_2/

Pan, J. (2017). How market dynamics of domestic and foreign social media firms shape strategies of internet censorship. *Problems of Post-Communism, 64*(3–4), 167–188.

Parliamentary Assembly. (2012, October 3). *The definition of political prisoner.* https://pace.coe.int/en/files/19150/html

Pepinsky, T. (2020). Authoritarian innovations: Theoretical foundations and practical implications. *Democratization, 27*(6), 1092–1101.

Politkovskaya, A. (2012). *Putin's Russia: The definitive account of Putin's rise to power.* Random House.

Przeworski, A., Alvarez, M. E., Cheibub, J. A., et al. (2000). *Democracy and development: Political institutions and well-being in the world, 1950–1990* (No. 3). Cambridge University Press.

Reimers, N., & Gurevych, I. (2019). Sentence-BERT: Sentence embeddings using siamese bert-networks. *arXiv preprint arXiv:1908.10084.*

Riquelme, F., & González-Cantergiani, P. (2016). Measuring user influence on Twitter: A survey. *Information Processing & Management, 52*(5), 949–975.

Ritter, E. H., & Conrad, C. R. (2016). Preventing and responding to dissent: The observational challenges of explaining strategic repression. *American Political Science Review, 110*(1), 85–99.

Robertson, G. (2013). Protesting Putinism. *Problems of Post-Communism, 60*(2), 11–23.

Rossman, E. (2022). Meet Russia's feminist resistance to Putin's war on Ukraine. *Green Left Weekly*, (1341), 13. https://search.informit.org/doi/10.3316/informit.393839445920891.

Roudakova, N. (2009). Journalism as "prostitution": Understanding Russia's reactions to Anna Politkovskaya's murder. *Political Communication, 26*(4), 412–429.

Rouvinsky, R. (2021). Lawmaking in times of domestic and foreign-policy instability (the Russian experience). *The Theory and Practice of Legislation, 9*(1), 117–139.

Sainz, O., & Rigau, G. (2021). Ask2transformers: Zero-shot domain labelling with pre-trained language models. *arXiv preprint arXiv:2101.02661.*

Schedler, A. (2013). *The politics of uncertainty: Sustaining and subverting electoral authoritarianism.* Oxford University Press.

Schock, K. (1999). People power and political opportunities: Social movement mobilization and outcomes in the Philippines and Burma. *Social Problems, 46*(3), 355–375.

Shahi, A., & Abdoh-Tabrizi, E. (2020). Iran's 2019–2020 demonstrations: The changing dynamics of political protests in Iran. *Asian Affairs, 51*(1), 1–41.

Shriver, T. E., & Adams, A. E. (2010). Cycles of repression and tactical innovation: The evolution of environmental dissidence in communist Czechoslovakia. *The Sociological Quarterly, 51*(2), 329–354.

Siegel, D. A. (2011). When does repression work? Collective action in social networks. *The Journal of Politics, 73*(4), 993–1010.

Skaaning, S.- E. (2021). *Lexical index of electoral democracy (LIED) dataset v6.0.* Harvard Dataverse.

Smith, W. (2011). Europe to the rescue: The killing of journalists in Russia and the European Court of Human Rights. *George Washington International Law Review, 43*, 493.

Snow, D. A., Vliegenthart, R., & Ketelaars, P. (2018). The framing perspective on social movements. In D. A. Snow, S. A. Soule, H. Kriesi, & H. J. McCammon (Eds.), *The Wiley Blackwell companion to social movements* (pp. 392–410). John Wiley & Sons.

Snyder, D. (1976). Theoretical and methodological problems in the analysis of governmental coercion and collective violence. *Journal of Political & Military Sociology, 4*(2), 277–293.

Sokirianskaia, E. (2005). Families and clans in Ingushetia and Chechnya: A fieldwork report. *Central Asian Survey, 24*(4), 453–467.

Sokirianskaia, E. (2023). *Bonds of blood?: State-building and clanship in Chechnya and Ingushetia.* Bloomsbury.

Sova. (2022). *About the centre Sova.* www.sova-center.ru/about-us/

SoVA Center. (2013). *Illegal use of anti-extremism legislation in Russia in 2012.* www.sova-center.ru/misuse/publications/2013/04/d26952/

Straughn, J. B. (2005). "Taking the state at its word": The arts of consentful contention in the German Democratic Republic. *American Journal of Sociology, 110*(6), 1598–1650.

Tarrow, S. (1993). Cycles of collective action: Between moments of madness and the repertoire of contention. *Social Science History, 17*(2), 281–307.

Tarrow, S. (2022). *Power in movement.* Cambridge University Press.

Tarrow, S. G. (1989). *Democracy and disorder: Protest and politics in Italy, 1965–1975.* Clarendon Press.

Taylor, V., & Van Dyke, N. (2004). "Get up, stand up": Tactical repertoires of social movements. In D. A. Snow, S. A. Soule, H. Kriesi (Eds.), *The Blackwell companion to social movements,* 262–293. Blackwell Publishing Ltd.

Tertytchnaya, K. (2023). "This rally is not authorized": Preventive repression and public opinion in electoral autocracies. *World Politics, 75*(3), 482–522.

The Guardian. (2014, December 30). *Kremlin critic Alexei Navalny given suspended sentence but brother jailed.* www.theguardian.com/world/2014/dec/30/kremlin-critic-navalny-given-suspended-sentence-brother-jailed

Tilly, C. (1993). Contentious repertoires in Great Britain, 1758–1834. *Social Science History, 17*(2), 253–280.

Tilly, C. (2010). *Regimes and repertoires.* University of Chicago Press.

Trejo, G. (2012). *Popular movements in autocracies: Religion, repression, and indigenous collective action in Mexico.* Cambridge University Press.

Trenin, D., Arbatov, A., Lipman, M., et al. (2012). *The Russian Awakening* (Tech. Rep.). www.jstor.org/stable/resrep13012

Van Laer, J., & Van Aelst, P. (2013). Cyber-protest and civil society: The internet and action repertoires in social movements. In Y. Jewkes & M. Yar (Eds.), *Handbook of internet crime* (pp. 230–254). Willan.

Van Stekelenburg, J., Klandermans, B., & Walgrave, S. (2018). Individual participation in street demonstrations. In D. A. Snow, S. A. Soule, H. Kriesi

(Eds.), *The Wiley Blackwell Companion to Social Movements*, 371. John Wiley & Sons.

Venice Commission. (2013, June 18). *Opinion on the issue of the prohibition of so-called "Propaganda of homosexuality" in the light of recent legislation in some Council of Europe Member States, adopted by the Venice Commission at its 95th Plenary Session (14–15 June 2013)* (Tech. Rep.). Council of Europe. www.venice.coe.int/webforms/documents/?pdf=CDL-AD(2013)022-e

Venice Commission. (2021). *Documents: Russia.* www.venice.coe.int/webforms/documents/default.aspx?country=26&other=true

Waller, J. M. (1993). Russia's legal foundations for civil repression. *Demokratizatsiya, 1*(3), 111.

Wang, D. J., & Soule, S. A. (2016). Tactical innovation in social movements: The effects of peripheral and multi-issue protest. *American Sociological Review, 81*(3), 517–548.

Wolchik, S. L. (2012). Can there be a color revolution? *Journal of Democracy, 23*, 63.

Wongngamdee, P. (2023). Propagating and resisting authoritarian innovation online: Thailand's 'rotc cyber' activity. In J. Ockey & N. S. Talib (Eds.), *Democratic recession, autocratization, and democratic backlash in southeast asia* (pp. 139–165). Palgrave Macmillan.

Xu, X. (2021). To repress or to co-opt? Authoritarian control in the age of digital surveillance. *American Journal of Political Science, 65*(2), 309–325.

Yabloko. (2021). *Registry of repressive laws of Russia.* www.yabloko.ru/cat-news/2021/09/16-1

Yaghi, M. (2018). Frame resonance, tactical innovation, and poor people in the Tunisian uprising. In P. G. Coy (ed.), *Research in social movements, conflicts and change* (Vol. 42, pp. 115–143). Emerald Group Publishing.

Yuen, S. (2023). The institutional foundation of countermobilization: Elites and pro-regime grassroots organizations in post-handover Hong Kong. *Government and Opposition, 58*(2), 316–337.

Zhang, H., & Pan, J. (2019). Casm: A deep-learning approach for identifying collective action events with text and image data from social media. *Sociological Methodology, 49*(1), 1–57.

Acknowledgments

As I was writing this Element, the Russian regime continued to intensify its repression against those fighting for change and civil liberties. Alexey Navalny's efforts to oppose the Kremlin led to actions by the regime that resulted in his death at the remote IK-3 maximum-security penal colony, far away from his family and supporters. Authorities cruelly refused to release his body to his mother for nine days, attempting to pressure her into agreeing to a funeral on their terms. The regime also detained hundreds of citizens who brought flowers to commemorate Navalny or gathered in protest.

The death of one of the Kremlin's most prominent critics, an activist, and politician who opposed the regime for over a decade, has inflicted further damage on the opposition and existing social movement organizations. Other leaders, such as Ilya Yashin or Vladimir Kara-Murza, face lengthy prison sentences and similar threats for their political participation and expressing their political beliefs together with tens of thousands of others who have been detained, persecuted, intimidated, injured, or killed for their views. At the same time, the regime has strengthened its rule, disregarding any voices advocating for freedoms and expressing their political beliefs. This reality underscores the brutality of authoritarian regimes and the repressive strategies they employ to ensure their longevity and silence dissent.

This Element would not have been possible without the courage of individuals like Navalny, who unite people against injustice. Those who continue to fight for change in Russia and similar regimes, despite constantly growing risks and repression, deserve more attention and unwavering support. By studying the strategies employed by authoritarian regimes, we can better understand how policies, methods of repression, and political decisions lead to the erosion of civil liberties. I hope this Element will encourage further research into the dynamics between ever-evolving authoritarian politics and contention, particularly focusing on innovative strategies these regimes use to ensure longevity.

I am immensely grateful to the series editors, David S. Meyer and Suzanne Staggenborg, for agreeing to work with me on this Element, supporting me throughout this process, and making it happen. My senior academic advisors and role models, Lee Morgenbesser and Ellie Martus, have accompanied me every step of the way, meticulously reading all drafts of this manuscript, providing crucial feedback, and assisting me throughout the writing process. Their guidance transformed the initial manuscript into what it is today, overcoming any challenges that arose along the way.

I am also thankful to the School of Government and International Relations at Griffith University for their support and for providing me with the necessary resources to complete this piece, including access to the HPC Gowonda cluster. Finally, I sincerely thank all my amazing colleagues who supported me in this endeavor and helped me manage the workload through their ceaseless encouragement and invaluable discussions.

Cambridge Elements ☰

Contentious Politics

David S. Meyer
University of California, Irvine

David S. Meyer is Professor of Sociology and Political Science at the University of California, Irvine. He has written extensively on social movements and public policy, mostly in the United States, and is a winner of the John D. McCarthy Award for Lifetime Achievement in the Scholarship of Social Movements and Collective Behavior.

Suzanne Staggenborg
University of Pittsburgh

Suzanne Staggenborg is Professor of Sociology at the University of Pittsburgh. She has studied organizational and political dynamics in a variety of social movements, including the women's movement and the environmental movement, and is a winner of the John D. McCarthy Award for Lifetime Achievement in the Scholarship of Social Movements and Collective Behavior.

About the series

Cambridge Elements series in Contentious Politics provides an important opportunity to bridge research and communication about the politics of protest across disciplines and between the academy and a broader public. Our focus is on political engagement, disruption, and collective action that extends beyond the boundaries of conventional institutional politics. Social movements, revolutionary campaigns, organized reform efforts, and more or less spontaneous uprisings are the important and interesting developments that animate contemporary politics; we welcome studies and analyses that promote better understanding and dialogue.

Cambridge Elements ≡

Contentious Politics

Printed in the United States
by Baker & Taylor Publisher Services